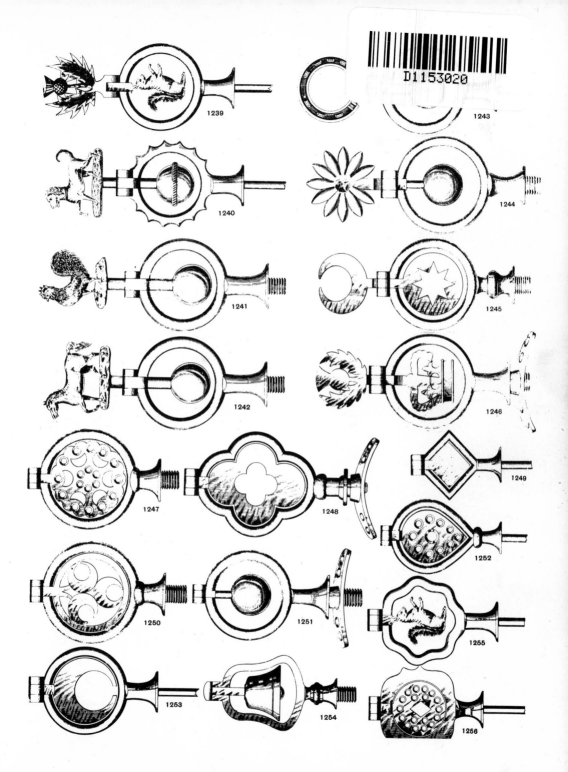

1239

1243

1240

1244

1241

1245

1242

1246

1247

1248

1249

1252

1250

1251

1255

1253

1254

1256

The Heavy Horse

ITS HARNESS AND HARNESS DECORATION

The Heavy Horse

ITS HARNESS AND HARNESS DECORATION

Terry Keegan

Line Drawings by G. A. KEEGAN

PELHAM BOOKS

Dedication
To my wife Mary, and Brian, Ricky, Roy and Alison.

First published in Great Britain by Pelham Books Ltd
52 Bedford Square
London, WC1
JUNE 1973
SECOND IMPRESSION APRIL 1974
THIRD IMPRESSION OCTOBER 1975
FOURTH IMPRESSION OCTOBER 1978

ISBN 0 7207 0560 6

Printed in Great Britain by Hollen Street Press Limited, Slough
and bound by Dorstel Press, Harlow

Contents

Illustrations

The Horse's Prayer

Feed me, water and care for me
And when the day's work is done,
Provide me with a clean shelter, a clean dry bed
And a stall wide enough for me to lie down in comfort;
Be always gentle to me, and talk to me;
Your voice often means more to me than the reins.
Pat me sometimes that I may serve you
The more gladly and learn to love thee. Do not jerk the reins,
And do not whip me when going up hill.
Never strike, beat, or kick me
When I do not understand what you mean,
But give me a chance to understand you.
Watch me, and if I fail to do your bidding,
See if something is wrong
With my harness, or my feet.
Don't draw the straps too tight.
Give me freedom to move my head.
If you insist on me wearing blinkers
To keep me from looking around, at least,
See to it that they do not press against my eyes.
Don't make my load too heavy,
And, don't leave me tied up in the rain.
Have me well shod,
Examine my teeth when I do not eat;
I may have an ulcerated tooth
And that you know is painful enough.
Do not tie my head in an unnatural position,
Or take away my best defence against flies
By cutting off my tail.
I cannot tell you when I'm thirsty
So please give me pure cold water frequently.
Do all you can to protect me from the sun
And throw a cover over me
When I am standing out in the cold.
Don't force an ice cold bit into my mouth,
But warm it first
In some warm water, or in your hands.
I always try to do cheerfully

The work you require of me.
And day and night
I stand for hours waiting for you.
And finally my master,
When my useful strength is gone,
Do not turn me out to starve or freeze,
Or sell me to a cruel owner
To be slowly tortured and starved to death.
But do thee my master take my life
In the kindest way.
And your God will reward you here and hereafter.
You may not think me irreverent
If I ask this in the name of
Him who was born in a stable.

AMEN

Supplied by A. E. Fisher, Benwick, Cambridgeshire.

Introduction

During my researches for material for this book, one correspondent made a strong plea for a book featuring the heavy horse as it is today, and the recent revival of interest in its future. My correspondent felt that too much of what had been written recently about the heavy horse was in the past tense and that the time had come for a book bringing the picture up to date.

For two years I have battled with the past and the present tenses and the past has come out the victor, principally because I discovered that so little of the great store of information which the older horsemen possess has ever been written down. As far as written matter is concerned, the heavy horse is the poor relation in the otherwise well documented horse world. Much has been written about the lighter carriage horse and how to harness and drive it, and possibly for this reason much of the working of the lighter driven horse became standard practice over the whole country.

Not so the heavy draught horse where harness and working practices varied, not only from county to county, but often from one district to another within those counties. Because the men who have this local knowledge are getting fewer and fewer, I believe there is a greater need to record this part of our social history than to write about the present efforts to retain and improve the status of the heavy horse in our society. There is a dearth of written information on the heavy horse harness, and most of the works produced on the decorations are simply catalogues of the patterns found of that hanging piece known as a horse brass.

A number of writers have covered the working of the heavy horse within a limited area. Ewart Evans did this admirably for part of Norfolk and Suffolk. But there was no book to be found comparing the different ways of working the horses over the country as a whole. As the information was there to be gathered, and the horsemen so willing to pass it on, I felt that the need for a book of this sort was greater than that suggested by my correspondent.

As the old harness about the farms gets destroyed, so more and more people are beginning to take an interest in it, not only from the decorative point of view, but also as a part of our social history. There are probably more people today who know what hames are than did thirty years ago, mainly because of their use by breweries as decoration for their public houses. Harness has begun to appear in the antique shops and it is being scattered far beyond its place of origin, so that in the future there is going to be a problem tracing the original area in which it was made. Already our museums are faced with this problem, and unless the harness-maker's name-plate is attached, there is difficulty in finding the area from which it originates.

It is hoped that this book will go some way towards helping to identify the chief characteristics of the harness patterns and the areas in which they were found.

Perhaps the past tense has come out on top, but there is still a great deal happening in the heavy horse world at the present moment and the signs are that even more will be happening in the future.

Clows Top, 1972   Terry Keegan

CHAPTER ONE

The Heavy Horse

HISTORY OF DEVELOPMENT IN BRITAIN

Until the latter half of the seventeenth century when new methods of warfare led to the abandonment of heavily armoured mounted soldiers, the development of the heavy horse in this country was limited almost entirely to military needs. The ox provided all the power needed to pull the plough and all the other draught requirement on the land, whilst the pack-horse and English nag carried the goods and passengers respectively along the appalling roads of the time.

For over 1000 years the English Great Horse was bred for purposes other than for commerce and agriculture. In the Middle Ages it became a military necessity to develop a horse more capable of carrying heavy weights of armour than could the native horses of the time. To achieve this, the heavy breeds already existing in Europe, such as the Flemish and Hainault horses, were introduced to this country. They were crossed with the native breeds to produce a horse more capable of carrying an armoured knight.

The greater the penetration power of weapons became, the heavier the armour required and the heavier still the horse that was required to carry these weights. Only the stoutest and largest animals were equal to the task. A knight in full armour, together with the horse's armour could weigh as much as 4 cwt, and it was in order to carry this burden that the Great Horse, or War Horse as it was also known, was developed in this country. Over the years many improvements were made, especially with introduced breeds from the continent.

Parliament passed a number of laws aimed at the breeding of bigger and better horses. An act of 1535 provided that all owners or farmers of 'parks and enclosed grounds to the extent of one mile in compass' should keep two mares able to bear foals 'of the height of thirteen handfuls'. There were penalties for those who allowed a mare to be sired by a stallion of 'under fourteen handfuls'.

In the reign of Edward VI, a law was passed prohibiting the importation of stallions less than 14 hands and of mares below 15 hands. Though these were probably minimum heights, it will nevertheless be evident that the armoured knights of the day rode into battle on a much smaller horse than the 17 and 18 hand giants of the nineteenth and twentieth centuries. The English Great

Horse had a long way to go before it reached the proportions of the showring heavies of today.

With the improvement of firearms and the consequent loss in popularity of armoured knights, the military necessity for the Great War Horse declined. From the middle of the seventeenth century the military need changed to one of a lighter, faster mount, and though a few breeders did carry on improvements, for nearly 100 years the Great Horse's numbers declined throughout the country.

The revival of interest in heavy horses came towards the end of the eighteenth century for two main reasons: first, efforts had been made to improve the surfaces of the roads, and with the increase in commerce a heavy draught animal was required to pull the large and cumbersome wagons of the day. The horse was found to perform this job better than the slow ox. Secondly, as agricultural practices improved and implements became lighter and more efficient, farmers also recognised the need to replace the slow, unwieldy teams of oxen by heavy horses.

The change was further encouraged by the breeding efforts of a number of notable improvers. Outstanding amongst these was Bakewell of Dishley, who was also famous for his improvements in sheep and cattle breeding. Bakewell crossed the Lincolnshire black horse with Dutch stallions, and Arthur Young, in 1786, writes of Bakewell's horses as 'the great heavy black, and his stallions are by far the finest I have ever seen of that breed. Nothing can be more compactly formed, and for all those farmers, but especially for those carriers and others whose teams must draw great weights, there cannot be a better breed than this'.

By the end of the eighteenth century there were as many horses as oxen in use. At this time much argument was put forward on merits of oxen and horses for draught purposes. From the thirteenth to the end of the eighteenth centuries, English agricultural writers had favoured the ox and many continued to do so as late as the middle of the nineteenth century.

The arguments in favour of oxen revolved round their cheapness to feed and harness, and the fact that, at the end of their useful draught life, they were still a capital asset to be sold for meat. It was also agreed that the ox was easier to train, less fussy over its food and less likely to be troubled with disease or physical ailments. But the most heated arguments were centred round its ability to pull. The ox men claimed that, though it may be slower, the ox team could pull steadier and was less likely to give up when faced with an extra difficult task.

The main arguments of the horsemen were that the horses were faster and more suited for the variety of jobs found about the farm. Also, it was unnecessary for horses to stop work to ruminate, as did the oxen. It was speed, coupled with the lighter designs of farm implements, that won the day for the horse. Speed became more and more important to the farmers as the enclosure of land proceeded and wages were being paid for all the work done. Oxen however continued to be used throughout the nineteenth century, and up to the First World War, there were a dozen or more teams at work in Sussex. The last team there, was not given up until as late as 1929.

By the beginning of the nineteenth century there had developed over the British Isles many different, but local, types of heavy draught horse. By the end of the century, for all practical purposes, the distinct breeds of heavy horse were the Shire, the Clydesdale and the Suffolk Punch. Though historians have credited each breed in turn as most representing the original war horse, it is most likely that each possesses some of the points of these early ancestors.

THE PRESENT DAY BREEDS

Devotees of each of the breeds formed societies in the 1870s to improve and promote their own particular champion. The Clydesdale and Suffolk societies were formed in 1877, followed closely by the Shire Horse Society in 1878.

We will take the native breeds in this order and consider them in further detail.

THE CLYDESDALE   This was the heavy horse of Scotland and the northern counties of England as far south as Durham on the east coast and the northern part of the Lake District on the west coast. The breed was first stabilised in the favourable breeding area of the Clyde Valley, especially in Lanarkshire. As early as the eighteenth century, stallions had been introduced to the native breeds from both Flanders and England, and the development of the modern Clydesdale, was due to this 'crossing of several horses of outstanding draught type with the heavy, thick, short legged, active native breeds found in Scotland' (*Standard Cyclopedia of Modern Agriculture*).

The formation of the Clydesdale Society in 1877 came about because the Scottish breeders wished to protect the Clydesdale breed from the introduction of horses of the Shire type. This was being done on a large scale by some Scottish breeders to obtain a heavier boned animal for work in the cities.

The first volume of the Clydesdale stud book describes the breed as follows:

Height—Average about 16·2 hands.

Colour—Fashionable colour brown, dark brown being preferred, whilst black and bay are also common. White markings on leg and face are regarded as a sign of purity of blood.

Head—A wide muzzle, large open nostrils, big ears, open forehead, broad between the eyes, which should be bright and intelligent.

Body—A massive neck, with shoulders slightly oblique. The withers should be high, the back short and the ribs well sprung from the backbone. Broad hindquarters with massive thighs.

Limbs—The slightly oblique shoulder does much to produce the long quick step for which the Clydesdale is so much admired; so does the strong forearm. The hocks should be broad and proportionately developed and the knees big. The feet should

The Clydesdale. Champion mare, Burdon Mira Beau, at the Great Yorkshire Show 1972, owned by H. Barron. Most popular on farms in Scotland and the North of England, the Clydesdale was also once used extensively in the cities being liked for its brisk action. (*Monty*)

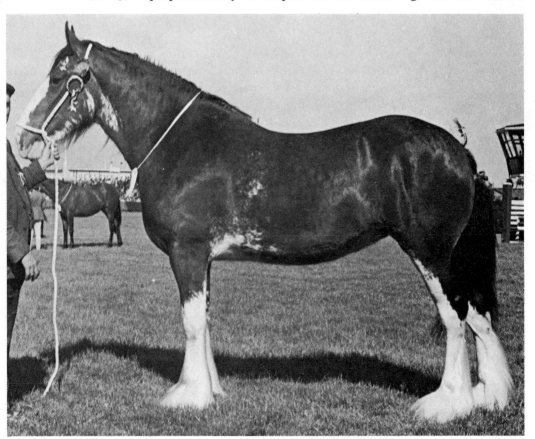

be round and open, the pasterns moderately sloped and of medium length—the hind ones being generally a little larger than the fore ones. The sinews of the leg should be thick, strong and thrown well back from the bone. The back of the leg from the knee down should have a fringe of silken hair.

Action—The movement of the Clydesdale should be active, with the forelegs placed well under the shoulders. The knees should be close, though not so close as to knock the knees together. The hind legs should also be planted closely together with the hocks turned slightly inwards, and the shanks plumb straight.

Improvements in the breed since the formation of the society included filling out the body more.

The Clydesdale is an ideal horse for both agricultural and town work. It was as a farmer's horse that it first earned its fame, a fame which created a great demand for the breed overseas, especially in the rapidly developing countries like New Zealand, Australia,

The Suffolk. Champion mare at Peterborough 1972, Euston Annabell, owned by Geo. Colson. The short legs in comparison to the size of its body, and the powerful shoulders and hindquarters, which gave the breed its amazing pulling ability, are evident in this illustration. (*Monty*)

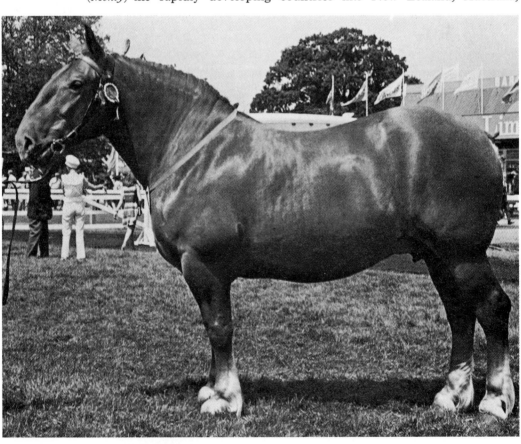

Canada and the United States of America. Exports of Clydesdales reached their highest in the late 1880s and again in 1906 and 1907, the demand being mainly for the USA, and Canada respectively.

As a commercial horse in the towns, the Clydesdale was at its best when between the shafts of the lighter delivery vans of the railways, where its fast moving action was at its greatest advantage.

THE SUFFOLK PUNCH   The Suffolk Punch has probably been of fixed type hundreds of years before our other native breeds of heavy horse. Certainly in the mid eighteenth century the Suffolk was a distinct race. Arthur Young, born in 1741, knew the breed well. Some authorities date it as far back as 1506, and it is even possible that its forebears were brought over by the Norsemen, who settled in the north eastern part of the country in the ninth century. It is East Anglia that is most associated with the Suffolk Punch, and in this area it reigned supreme. All Suffolk Punches in existence today are said to be direct descendants in the male line of a Lincolnshire trotting stallion born in 1768 and known as Crisp's horse of Ufford.

General—The chief characteristics of the Suffolk are his great drawing power, unusual docility, activity and longevity. They possess an iron constitution and immense powers of endurance.

Colour—Various shades of chestnut (the spelling 'chesnut' is often traditionally used when linked with the Suffolk horse) from a very dark mahogany to a bright golden colour. A white star is often found on the face. Manes and tails are lighter than the rest of the body.

Size—Height varies from $15\frac{3}{4}$ to $16\frac{1}{2}$ hands, and weight from 1900 to 2240 lb.

Head—Big head with broad forehead carried well forward, with a spirited appearance.

Body—Long and muscular shoulders well thrown back at the withers and a deep neck at the collar, arched gracefully towards the head. The body is deep, round and compact, looking a little too heavy for the short, clean legs. A wide chest, giving plenty of room between the forelegs. Hindquarters—powerful.

Limbs—Short in comparison to the massive body, but should be straight with big knees and free from coarse hair. Pasterns strong with bone of compact quality and feet of good size.

Action—Walk, smart and true; trot well balanced and with good action.

Of the first twenty-three shows of the Royal Agricultural Society of England, Suffolks took fourteen first prizes for the best horse suited for agricultural purposes, and about as many second prizes, but after this initial period of success, the Suffolk lost its superiority to the other breeds. The faults that were supposed to be responsible for this were unsound feet, tendency towards being calf-kneed, and a lack of bone beneath the knee. These faults are not prevalent in the pure bred Suffolk of today.

The Suffolk is best suited for agricultural work, but has also worked well in the streets of most of the cities in the southern part of Britain. The immense power of the Suffolk is partly accounted for by the low position of the shoulder, which enables the horse to throw so much of his weight into the collar. Their ability to tug at a dead pull led to their popularity in the drawing matches. Their longevity was renowned, and cases have been known where Suffolk mares have gone on breeding when upwards of thirty years old. One well known stallion was advertised as a stud horse for twenty-five years. Another characteristic of the breed is its ability to do well on an allowance of food insufficient for other breeds.

THE SHIRE   Leicestershire, Staffordshire and Derbyshire in the heart of England seem to be the areas most favoured as breeding the ancestors of the modern Shire. Lincolnshire too produced its contribution to the breed, as did many other areas. But the black horses of Derbyshire in the middle of the eighteenth century provide the earliest records of the breed in the stud books. A black stallion by the unlikely name of 'the Packington Blind Horse' has the honour of being the earliest recorded, though studs of black horses were well known before his birth in 1755.

As mentioned earlier, Robert Bakewell did much to improve and champion the breed in the latter part of the eighteenth century. Its development into the heaviest breed in the draught horse world was checked for a time by the R.A.S.E. advocating a lighter type of draught horse for farm work. By the middle of the nineteenth century, however, the demand for massive, powerful horses returned—especially for commercial work.

The English Cart Horse Society was formed in 1878 for the establishment of a stud book for Shire bred horses and to improve and promote the breed. Six years later the title was changed to the Shire Horse Society. A list of points for the breed was drawn up, though this has been amended to meet modern requirements. The most notable amendment was the dropping of the need to have a profusion of hair, or feather, on the legs. Today's requirement is for a cleaner legged horse with finer, silky hair.

The present day scale of points is as follows:

General—The shire should possess strength, a good constitution, stamina, power, docility and adaptability. His purpose in life is to pull weight, and immense power in his frame makes him ideally suited for this task.

Colour—Black, brown, bay or grey.

Size—Height from 16½ to 17½ hands. Stallions and geldings weigh from one ton to 22 cwt, and mares a bit less.

Head—Lean in proportion to the body, forehead broad between the eyes. Eyes large, prominent and docile in expression; thin nostrils and slightly roman nosed; ears long and lean.

Body—Shoulders deep and oblique; neck fairly long and slightly arched; back strong, muscular and short, chest wide and legs well under the body; hindquarters long and sweeping, wide and muscular; ribs round, deep and well sprung.

Limbs—Long and muscular arms, legs big and massive; knees square and large, sinews hard and clear of the cannon bones; feet deep, not too wide, and open at the heels; feather—not too much—fine, straight and silky.

The Shire. Heaton Majestic, owned by J. & W. Whewell, winner at Peterborough in 1972. The largest breed of horse in the world, the Shire is renowned for its strength. The modern Shire is a cleaner-legged horse than 30 years ago with only a small amount of feather.
(Monty)

Action—Stallions go with force, using both knees and hocks. He should go straight and true before and behind. Geldings should be very active and gay movers and should look like, and be able to do, a full day's work.

The Shire horse is ideally suited for commercial draught work. In the past they bore the brunt of the work done in drays and coal carts in the cities and the timber and farm wagons on the land. They proved themselves very adaptable to all kinds of work in town and country. They are built for strength and hard work and over the years many were exported to satisfy the demand from overseas. America bought a large number in the ten years after the formation of the Society, and is still importing small numbers to this day. Other countries to which the breed was extensively exported included Canada, Australia and Germany.

The Shire is a good doer and well suited to our climatic conditions. In general they are very docile and easily controlled.

THE PERCHERON   The Percheron is not a native breed and arrived in this country late in the heavy horse scene. After some unsuccessful introductions at the beginning of the century, it was eventually established after the First World War. During the war, many of the soldiers from Britain who fought on the western front made contact with the Percheron breed as remounts and in gun-carriage teams. They were impressed by the docility of the breed and the ease with which the horses could be trained and worked. Many were imported to Britain during the war and many more arrived with the glut of horses after the war finished. Soon after the war, the British Percheron Horse Society was formed to promote the breed and form a stud book.

The Percheron originates from the Perche district of France, 75 miles south east of Paris, and like its British counterparts, was originally bred as a war horse. The heavy draught Percheron as we know it today was developed about the early part of the nineteenth century. From the middle of the century many were exported to America where they became one of the most popular breeds for heavy draught work.

The British Percheron Society list the breed characteristics as follows:

General—The British Percheron horse is essentially a heavy draught animal possessing great muscular development combined with style and activity. It should possess ample bone of good quality and give a general impression of balance and power.

Colour—Grey or black, with a minimum of white. Skin and coat should be of fine quality.

Size—Stallions should be not less than 16·3 hands high and mares 16·1, but width and depth must not be sacrificed to height at maturity. Stallions weigh 18 to 20 cwt, and mares 16 to 18 cwt.

Head—Wide across the eyes, which should be full and docile; ears medium in size and erect; deep cheek, curved on lower side and not long from eye to nose; intelligent expression.

Body—Strong neck, not short; full arched crest in the case of stallions; wide chest and deep, well laid shoulders; back strong and short; ribs wide and deep, deep at flank; hindquarters of exceptional width and long from hips to tail.

Limbs—Strong arms, full second thighs, big knees and broad hocks. Bone, heavy and flat, cannons short, and pasterns of medium length. Feet of reasonable size, of good quality hard, blue horn. Limbs as clean and free from hair as possible.

The Percheron. Histon Limelight, owned by Baily & Son, best stallion at Peterborough in 1972. A relative newcomer to this country from France, the Percheron has many similar characteristics to our native Suffolk. (*Monty*)

Action—Straight, bold and with a long, free stride. Hocks well flexed and kept close.

Although its successful introduction into Britain was late, the Percheron soon achieved popularity and was used for most kinds of heavy horse work, though it was most popular when working on the land. The general appearance of the heavy type of Percheron is similar to that of the Suffolk and, like the latter, it carries no feather.

Other breeds of heavy draught horse were introduced into this country from time to time, especially the black Belgian horses so loved for funerals by undertakers.

INTERBREED RIVALRY

So far an attempt has been made to steer clear of arguments in praise of one breed against another. The bare bones of each breed have been described, but there is a lot of meat to be found in the praises sung by each Society for their own breed against others, and the down to earth comments from the men who worked amongst them.

The Percheron was either simply dismissed as a foreigner, or else the breed had not been long enough established in this country to have built up a lot of argument one way or another. Some say that it was only the popularity of the grey colouring that established the breed in this country. At that time the Shire was not producing good greys and as the only native grey was the Shire, the tendency was for the grey colouring to die out.

The Percheron came in for some criticism of not being able to stand up to the rigours of heavy haulage in our towns and cities as well as could the native breeds. A high percentage were said to suffer azoturia—a condition caused when horses are fed up well for supreme fitness and then kept from working by holiday periods. The result is stiffness and pain.

The Suffolk breed never reached the popularity one would have expected from a horse achieving the show successes it gained in the middle of the last century. The breed succeeded in dominating that part of the country from where it originated. The breed seldom achieved the status of general farm horse outside East Anglia. Most of those that left the area were on the estates of big landowners, where, it seems, they were more often kept for their appearance than for any other reason. Big estates often took a pride in having all matching horses to run the farms. One such estate, the Lowther estate in Westmorland, went to great lengths to build up a stud of chestnut Suffolks because, it is said, they best matched the yellow trimmings of which the 'Yellow Earl' (he was the first president of the A.A.) was so fond. The home farms on some of the big Scottish estates favoured stables full of matching black horses, and when black Clydesdales could not be found, the black Belgians were imported to satisfy this colour preference.

But not everyone decided on the type of horse best suited for their purposes by its colour alone. The clean legs of both Percheron and Suffolk helped a great deal towards making these breeds popular, especially with the horsemen who worked them, in areas of wet, heavy clays. They were also preferred for row crop work because of their smaller feet. They did less damage to the plants in market gardens than the bigger breeds.

Like the Percheron, the Suffolk came in for a lot of criticism when working on the streets of busy cities. They often developed contracted and brittle feet, and arthritis of the fetlock joints, and ringbone (new bone growth on the surface of the original bone, causing lameness) was also common. The cobbled streets of our towns and cities were a severe testing ground for the feet of any breed, and without good feet suited to the road conditions a horse was useless.

For longevity, however, the Suffolk was superior to the other breeds. Some were known to survive the rigours of commercial street working for over twenty years, and as the average for all breeds in city working, was probably less than seven years, at least some Suffolks had sound useful feet!

Another praise often sung in the Suffolk's favour was the fact that they were 'good doers'. It took less to feed a Suffolk than any of the other breeds—thriving better on long hours and short rations.

But most of all, it was the ability of the Suffolk to pull in the collar when other breeds would give up, that figured in the arguments put forward by the breed's supporters against rival breeds. Youatt, writing in the middle of the last century, illustrated this point:

'The excellence, and a rare one, of the old Suffolk consisted in nimbleness of action, and the honesty and continuance with which he would exert himself at a dead pull. Many a good draught horse knows well what he can effect; and, after he has attempted it and failed, no torture of the whip will induce him to strain his powers beyond their natural extent. The Suffolk, however, would tug at a dead pull until he dropped.'

SHIRE v CLYDESDALE

There are more heated arguments in the interbreed rivalry of the Shire and Clydesdale than between any of the other breeds. After sifting through all the points for and against one cannot help agreeing with the view of a writer to the *Livestock Journal* who, in 1922, wrote of the interbreed rivalry, and that in his view 'the blend of the two horses is the best dray horse in the world and unbeaten'. And this seems to be the direction in which the two breeds have moved since that date.

Many horsemen argue that there is little difference between the two breeds today; so much so that one recent winner of a Shire gelding class at the Royal Show suggested that 'they are all crosses today and both the Shire and Clydesdale stud books want burning!'.

Perhaps we could picture a scene at the rails of the collecting ring at a show. Shires and Clydesdales are parading and standing around on the lush turf waiting their turn to enter the main arena. A Clydesdale devotee and a Shire devotee find themselves leaning on the rail, shoulder to shoulder, watching the heavy horse scene. The conversation between them is imaginary, but helps to set out most of the arguments one hears for and against the two breeds. It starts with Mr. Clydesdale eyeing the above mentioned gelding and saying half to himself, but really for the benefit of those around him:

'Ye canna say that yon horse is a Shire. It has mair Clydesdale aboot it than any other breed. They Shire men must at last hae seen how much better are the qualities of the Clydesdale.'

Mr. Shire hears it all, as he was meant to, and though his temperature rises noticeably, he refrains from commenting for some time. His eyes follow the general direction of Mr. Clydesdale's critical stare, and he cannot help agreeing inwardly that the breed has changed over the years, mainly through the introduction of Clydesdale blood. However, he isn't to be outdone and his desire is to hit back where it hurts most.

'I do believe,' he reflects aloud, 'that when the Scots decided to form their stud book in 1876 most of the best Clydesdales of the day had been bred out of good Shire mares to increase their size and strength.' He has exaggerated, on purpose, and takes his opponent by surprise.

Mr. Clydesdale reddens a little but keeps his eyes on the mountains of taut muscles lining up to go into the ring. Then he challenges, 'Did any Clydesdale ever need the weight of a Shire to pull the same load along?'

Mr. Shire takes up the challenge, 'It's an indisputable fact that your Clydesdale, generally speaking, lacks the power which the Shire possesses for pulling or backing a loaded wagon.'

The last of the braided tails disappears into the main ring and the crowd begins to drift away.

Mr. Clydesdale keeps his eye on the closed gate of the ring and slowly, but deliberately, replies: 'Brains and spirit, brains and spirit; they are of more consequence than mere weight. A horse must be able to pull by sheer dint of will. In the breeding of Clydesdales the factors of brains and spirit are as much taken into account as weight.'

A brief interruption from an interested spectator from Wales: 'The half-legged Welsh cart-horse would skin a Clydesdale at pulling. Especially if the ground were soggy, being lower down, he could get down and draw better than any long legged horse could.'

'I still say,' interrupts Mr. Shire, 'a good heavy horse is far better than a good light one from the draught horse users point of view.'

'Aye,' murmurs Mr. Clydesdale rather irrelevantly, 'and the bigger the horse the more likely he is to have trouble and become unsound.'

'Well that would certainly apply to the Clydesdales big flat feet. They didn't survive the cobbled city streets very well, and what is more,' Mr. Shire warms to the occasion, 'the length and obliquity of the pasterns so often seen in the Clydesdale predisposes to ring-bone, which frequently develops before it is long on the streets.'

'Well, whilst we are on the subject of legs and feet,' Mr. Clydesdale hits back, 'whatever happened to yon whinbushes you used to find round the Shire's legs, so that they could hardly put one foot in front of the other?'

Mr. Shire draws breath to answer, but his words are pushed aside.

'And all the troubles it caused; all the bother with greasy feet; the constant stamping in the stable throughout the night; and the smell! How the ploughmen used to curse those hairy legs, especially when working on heavy clay! You would wonder how the Shire Society believed for so long that this hair was supposed to be an indication of quality, substance and ruggedness. And the way those show lads used to turn them out with the hair all stiff with resin to make them look even hairier—just to suit the judges!'

Mr. Shire feels it is time to put a halt to this line of fire: 'The modern Shire,' he informs Mr. Clydesdale, 'has been bred for some years now with only a small amount of fine silky hair on the legs . . .'

'Aye, and it took the Clydesdale to bring that about,' triumphs the man from the North. 'Even before the Shire Society recognised the need for getting rid of the old besom legs, Shire breeders were bringing their mares to Scotland to be covered by Clydesdales—and they never let on at first!'

'The modern Shires,' repeats Mr. Shire, 'are being bred with far less hair than before, by the judicious choice of sire and dam, and you never hear of grease troubles today.'

'Aye, and it also needed the Clydesdale blood to hurry the Shire up a bit. He was always too slow. A Clydesdale, he is more active in his work. He could even out-trot many hacks.'

'That may be so, and I'll admit to too much Clydesdale being introduced into the breed, resulting in a smaller, lighter horse, but in the past, in all the big cities it was the Shire which figured most prominently in the stables of the big horse users. And another thing; the Shire was so much easier to break into harness.'

'But wait a minute!' Mr. Clydesdale sounds a little hurt. 'The Clydesdale maybe needs a bit more skill to break in, and we Scots have that skill, but because they are more fiery and spirited, this must be to their credit. A spirited horse is always a more intelligent horse.'

'I'd call it bad temper. It is rarely one finds a bad tempered Shire, and yet they are noted for their intelligence.'

'Well, intelligence will not be of much use to them if they only

Scene at the Shire Horse Society's show at the Agricultural Hall, Islington in 1886. The Society was formed in 1878 to improve and promote the breed. With a membership today of over 1,000 the Society, now holds its annual spring show at Peterborough Showground.
(*Radio Times Hulton*)

last seven or eight years on the road. The Clydesdale lasts much longer, and was often seen still doing its job at twenty-two and twenty-three years of age.'

'Shire are just as long lived . . ..'

The argument breaks down into a mild slanging match. Pulling power, activeness, the problems of hairy legs and many more subjects are frequently heard. The return of the equine giants from the ring breaks up the argument. And as they part, two or three of the interested bystanders, who had been listening intently to both sides, reached agreement amongst themselves—that the best draught horse to be found in the world was neither Shire nor Clydesdale, but a good cross of the two breeds, and, but for the fads of the show ring, neither breed would have survived separately. In fact, many horsemen have held for years that there is no difference between the breeds, and when first class specimens of each are stood side by side, it would be difficult to tell which was which.

Although the majority of farm horses had the general appearance of one or other of the breeds, they were mainly horses of varied ancestry that showed a mixture of character. In many areas, especially those of small farms, it would be difficult to find a single horse that could have been admitted to one or other of the stud books. They were simply called cart-horses and carried out the work expected of them to the satisfaction of their owners.

At one time the standard of these mixed cart-horses was very poor, but as the different breeds were developed and improved, stallions from the recognised breeds were brought to the farms to cover the cart-horse mares. In this way the general standard was improved. Specialist breeders would travel their stallions in the district, announcing the dates on which the stallion was to be available in each area. Some districts formed their own societies, banding together to hire annually the best available stallion for the use of their own members. Scotland was the forerunner of the formation of these horse hiring societies, some records going back to the 1830s. Stallions were hired originally at special stallion shows (the Glasgow stallion show being one of the most famous), but later private hirings replaced the shows. Each society would hire a stallion and charge its members a fixed sum for the use of its services.

THE END OF THE HEAVY HORSE ERA

The era of the heavy horse was at its peak just prior to the First World War. By 1911, although the tram horses had been replaced by electric traction, and the internal combustion engine was eating into the numbers of bus and cab horses as well as the lighter van horses, for the heaviest types of work the position of the horse was as yet virtually unchallenged. Up to that time there were very few heavy lorries that were a commercial success.

The steam engine had been the first mechanical source of power to really challenge the horse, but although the railway took over the distant carriage of goods around the country, they in fact created more work for the heavy horses than they had taken away. Railway companies were some of the largest users of horses—for short haul work. Steam power was used on the land as early as 1820, in the Lothians and Northumberland, and steam engines gradually took over the work of driving the threshing engines. Steam for ploughing became widely used during the second half of the nineteenth century, but the engines were too cumbersome to challenge seriously the position of the horse.

It was the speeding up of the development of the internal combustion engine during the First World War, mainly in America, which finally provided a superior form of manœuvreable power to the heavy horse. The constant need for horses at the war front robbed the farms of a lot of their power, and many farmers sought mechanical means to help them achieve the increase in production demanded from the land.

After the war there was a glut of horses returning from military service and prices fell. The bottom fell out of the market for the breeders and many gave up. But by 1925 there was such a shortage of home bred horses that many were imported from Europe, especially the Percheron breed.

Motor lorries and tractors slowly improved in power and reliability and the number of operators giving up using horses rose annually.

One of the deciding factors for the change from horse to tractor came from an unexpected quarter—disease amongst the horses. The disease became known as 'grass sickness' and to this day its cause continues to baffle the veterinary world. In the early 1920s it reached epidemic proportions on the large farms lying on the eastern side of Scotland, and the entire horse population was almost wiped out.

Mr. Marshall Manson of Brechin described how the disease first appeared at the nearby Yeomanry camp at Barry amongst the horses returning from the continent. From there it spread to the surrounding farms and soon the horse population was decimated. It became impossible to insure horses against grass sickness, and although every sort of cure was tried, the deaths continued. For years the grass itself was suspect, but even pit-ponies which had never been up for grass, became afflicted. Farmers who persisted in the fight were losing as many as eight to ten horses each year, till eventually they gave up the struggle and turned to mechanical power to work their farms.

Angus was probably the worst hit area, but the disease spread over the whole of the British Isles, and no doubt hastened the change over to the use of tractors in many other areas.

By the time the Second World War had plunged Europe into darkness once more, the tractor and heavy lorry had well and truly gained the upper hand. The demand for greatly increased food production during the war could not be adequately achieved by the small reserves of labour and horse power left on the land, so machines were brought in to do the job, and the machines have stayed ever since.

A small nucleus of horse users kept their stables going during the difficult post-war period, and many, supported by their own enthusiasm and that of the breed societies, have managed to survive to the present day and to see a renewed interest in the use of heavy horses for both commercial and farm work. Sound economic reasons have been put forward in this age of work study and computer programs for the retention of the heavy horse for short haul delivery work in our towns and cities. This has been made possible by the high cost of tax and insurance for motor vehicles, and also by the slowing up of traffic on the crowded city streets.

Brewery companies are very much to the fore in the fight to retain the heavy horse, and those that have kept their stables going, are finding it an increasingly profitable operation, especially if the horses are used on deliveries within a five mile radius of the brewery. But one Midland brewery continues to run down its stables for a number of reasons which highlight the problems faced by those working horses in modern traffic conditions. Firstly, complicated one-way systems have increased mileages, and the increase in the number of traffic lights has added to the amount of stopping and starting imposed on the horses. Active discouragement of the use of horses in certain busy thoroughfares by the authorities, and the risk of injury to the horses by collision with other road users, and also by increased pollution of the atmosphere, is on the increase. But most of all there is lack of enthusiasm amongst the staff to keep the horses going.

More than any other factor, it is the enthusiasm for the horse that has kept it in use today, and as people's enthusiasm grows so they are introducing more heavy horses back on to the land and on to the streets, and particularly back into the middle of the show ring.

CHAPTER TWO

The History of Harness

THE YOKE AND EARLY METHODS OF HARNESSING

The first horses domesticated by man about 4000 years ago were like small ponies, too lightly built to carry much weight. For this reason the horse started its long service to mankind yoked to a conveyance of some sort in a similar manner to the already domesticated ox. For many years before the horse was broken to harness, the ox had been pulling rudimentary ploughs and wheeled vehicles. The method developed for harnessing the ox to its work was the yoke and, although thousands of developing years of civilisation have passed by, the same method of harnessing is still in use in many parts of the world, including some modern, developed countries.

The yoke is simply a baulk of timber firmly attached to a pair of oxen and to which a plough or vehicle can be conveniently coupled. The yoke can be attached either by lashing it to the horns of the oxen or by fixing it against their high shoulders by passing a frame of some sort through the yoke and round the neck of the oxen to hold it in that position. For 5000 years oxen have worked very satisfactorily harnessed in this manner, and though in the last 200 years many attempts were made to work oxen in padded collars, as in this country, or in rudimentary wooden collars as in northern Europe, those that are still to be found working have retained the method developed in the earliest civilisations.

It was natural that the earliest harness worked out for the first domesticated horses should be on the same lines as that of the oxen, and for the next 2000 years, until the end of the Roman Empire, the horse was harnessed to its load by a yoke placed on top of its withers. This arrangement may have proved ideal for the ox, but unfortunately the horse is not built in the same way, particularly in not having the high shoulders of the ox, against which the yoke could be placed.

This would be a good point at which to try and explain how a horse best uses its power to pull a load, and having done this, to relate it to the history of the development of horse harness. The beautifully complicated collection of flesh, bone, muscle and sinew combine to make the horse an ideal beast for using its own weight to move even greater weights by the use of harness.

Explained in a simple form, a horse pulls best from a point just in front of the shoulders and in line with its own centre of gravity and the centre of resistance of the object to be pulled. Thus in Fig. 1, if G is the centre of gravity of the horse and R1 the centre of resistance of the plough, the ideal pulling point—or point of draught—is at A1 in front of the shoulders and in line with points G and R1. If the centre of resistance rises to R2, then the ideal point of draught moves to A2.

This movement of the ideal point of draught from A1 to A2 will be further discussed in the chapter covering hames and shifting draught hooks, but for the purpose of this chapter suffice is to say that the horse pulls at its best when coupled to its load at a point just forward of the shoulders in the vicinity of points A1 and A2.

Returning to the yoke as a method of coupling the horse to its load, if point Y on the diagram represents the point at which the yoke was fixed, it will be seen that it was sited too high for the horse to pull most efficiently.

The harnessed horse was first used extensively for pulling two-wheeled war chariots attached to the yoke by a centre pole. The use of two, three and sometimes four horses to pull these relatively light vehicles at speed meant that the loss of some pulling power, through the use of the yoke, was of little importance. The biggest problem was how to keep the yoke firmly in position on the horse's withers. Probably the best way of doing this was described by Homer in the Iliad (Fig. 2). He explains the mode of harnessing the horses at the seige of Troy 3000 years ago.

From the yoke a simple strap of several thicknesses of leather went round the horse's neck to serve as a rudimentary collar. From

Fig 1
Simplified diagram of
the points of draught
horse harness

A1, A2 Ideal point of draught
R1, R2 Centre of resistance
G Centre of gravity of horse

Y Point of draught of yoke
B Point of draught of breast collar

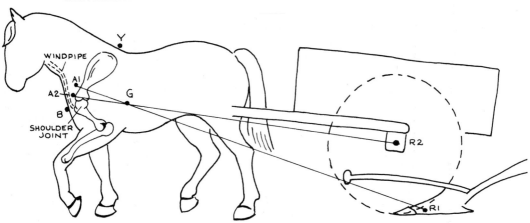

Fig 2
Harnessing to a yoke on
top of the horse's
withers. 1000 BC

the same point of the yoke a second strap passed round the body of
the horse rather like a girth and was fixed to the neck strap at the
withers. When pulling hard in the yoke, to prevent the neck strap
rising up the horse's throat and pressing on its windpipe, a strap
was fixed to the bottom of the neckstrap and passed between the
front legs, to be coupled to the girth, rather in the fashion of the
modern cart-horse martingale.

A pair of horses were thus yoked together to the chariot and
neither traces nor breeching were needed in this form of harness.
If a third or fourth horse were attached, they were coupled either
side by means of a single trace from a simple neck strap. Commenting
on these neck straps, Youatt in *The Horse*, 1851, writes: 'These
straps, if well fitted, were not bad; but as they must have pressed
in some degree upon the throat, they could not be equal to the
collars of the yoked horses, still less to the collar at present used.'

The yoke was later designed to give a better fit to the horse's
neck by curving the ends, and also by attaching curved side pieces
which fitted round the horse's neck rather like a collar. This undoubtedly helped to keep the yoke fixed on the horse's withers,
but the point of traction was still too high. As long as light vehicles,
running on relatively level ground free from obstructions, were all
that was required, this system of harnessing was sufficient.

The first development of the modern breast collar came in Roman
times when the two outside horses attached to the chariot were
each provided with double traces which met in front of the horse's
shoulders. Instead of the diagonal neck strap, the traces were now
horizontal and kept in place by a girth strap and pad. They were
attached to the chariot by a form of swingle-tree. Breast collars of
this type are in use today in many parts of the world on both heavy
and light harness horses.

Although the breast collar represents a great improvement in the
positioning of the point of traction, it will be seen from Fig. 1 that,

if B represents that point, it is nearly correct for pulling a vehicle with a high centre of resistance (R2), but is too low for any work with a lower centre (R1). Two other disadvantages of the breast collar show up in the diagram. In the first place it passes over the joint of the horse's shoulder and tends to interfere with its action, and secondly, unless firmly anchored to the girth strap, it tends to rise on the throat and restrict the horse's windpipe, especially when the horse is pulling hard.

Once the horse was bred strong enough to carry mounted soldiers into battle, the more restricted chariot lost its popularity.

The Romans did build roads suitable for heavy vehicles, but the ox and its yoke were more suited for this kind of work, and for nearly 1000 years the horse was little used in harness. As we saw in Chapter One, the heavy horse was bred as a war horse for carrying armoured knights into battle. Smaller horses were used for carrying goods about the country. The few roads were unsuitable for anything but the pack horse trains, whilst in the fields the ox, yoked in teams, continued to pull the heavy ploughs.

THE DEVELOPMENT OF MODERN HARNESS

By the beginning of the 19th century there were as many horses as oxen in use on the land, and though W. H. Pyne's series of drawings show horses of that time to be on the light side, they were still faster than oxen. The harness has changed little since then, but the decoration of wool fringing on the housen later gave way to brass over much of the harness. (M.E.R.L)

Although the neck collar existed in rudimentary form in Roman times, and the Chinese are said to have used it about the same period, it was little seen in Europe until the tenth century when it reappeared in rigid padded form much as it exists today. The development of shafts instead of a single pole, enabled a single horse to pull a vehicle, and the padded collar became the means of attaching the horse to its draught. The collar supported rigid frames—called hames—to take the draught. The collar also sat on the shoulders in such a way that it did not interfere with the horse's breathing, nor with the movement of its shoulders, and enabled the horse to throw all its weight into pulling. Most important of all, the collar finally provided a means of attaching the horse to its draught at a point which gave it its optimum ability to pull.

To take the weight of the shafts on the horse's back and to reduce chafing, a padded cart saddle was developed simultaneously with the development of shafts. So too was a simple form of breeching to act as a form of brake.

The slow pace of oxen meant that there was no need for the development of control of the animal by reins. From the earliest days of control has been effected by a man walking beside the animals and talking to them, or goading them forward or to one side or another when necessary. Oxen are quick to learn and words of command are soon obeyed.

The horse, however, was harnessed for use at much faster speeds, and the driver had to ride the chariots to keep control. A system of control through the use of a bit in the horse's mouth—probably first made of rope—and reins, was developed early. To hold the bit firmly in the mouth a simple form of head bridle was needed and, apart from the introduction of metal bits, for over 3000 years the harnessed horse was controlled by this simple arrangement of bridle, bit and reins.

It was probably the development of horse armour for the heavy war horse that started the practice of limiting the horse's vision. At first this was most likely by way of protection against injury during battle, but for some unknown reason the practice continued long after horse armour had been discarded. To this day most of the heavy horses in Britain, and in most overseas countries, are blinkered to limit their vision. The arguments for and against the use of blinkers are discussed in the following chapter, but suffice it to say that there are also many areas where horses are used without wearing blinkers, and control by rein and bit is equally as effective.

The check rein, or bearing rein, seems to have been an early development. Representations of bearing reins attached to the yoke are seen in early sculptures of the harnessed horse. The bearing rein works on the principle that, the faster a horse runs, the farther it needs to stretch out its neck, and the bearing rein was probably introduced to prevent the horses from taking all control from the driver's hands. They could also have been used to keep individual horses pulling within the power of the rest of the team.

Fig 3
A 14th Century illustration from the Luttrell Psalter showing horses harnessed in line and wearing the basic essentials of modern heavy horse harness

The bearing rein acts in a similar way to a governor on an engine. According to its adjustment, it can restrict the power of the animal by not allowing it to stretch its neck to its best advantage. This is the purpose for which it was probably originally intended or maybe to keep the horse from turning its head too much to the left or right, but the inhuman practice of tightening bearing reins for the sole purpose of forcing the horse to arch its neck as high fashion dictated

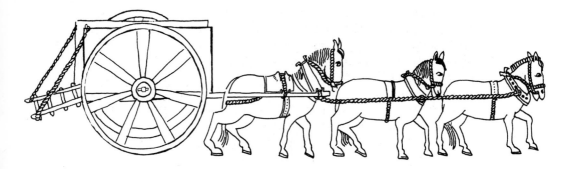

Three of Mr. Ovendens team of four Shires at the Thanet ploughing Championships in 1951. Note the wooden hames, rope traces, and the stretch stick to keep each pair of horses evenly spaced. The narrow decorated breaststrap is typical of the area. The mud collecting on the hair round the horse's feet often led to the condition known as grease. (M.E.R.L)

it should, is a relatively modern madness of mankind. The arguments for and against bearing reins are further discussed in the next chapter.

The development of shafts also meant re-arranging the method of attaching additional power to the vehicle. In the days of the yoke, extra power was given to the chariots by adding horses at the side of those in the yoke. In this way there could be up to four horses abreast. Once a single horse was used in shafts, it became more suitable to attach an additional horse in front of or in line with the shaft horse, by the use of traces attached to the ends of the shafts.

The use of a number of horses pulling in line in this fashion, only appears from the Middle Ages onwards. The traces were originally made of rope, as was much of the rest of the harness—such as, backbands for holding the shafts over the saddle, bellybands to stop the shafts of a two-wheeled cart from tipping and, of course, the reins (Fig. 3).

Although chains mostly replaced ropes on the heavy horse harness over 100 years ago, there are parts of eastern Kent where even to this day, rope traces attached to wooden hames are still in regular use.

Rope making was often closely associated with the harness-

James Stewart Del.

Edw.d Hacker Sc.

SINGLE PLOUGH HARNESS.

DOUBLE HORSE CART.

As the design of implements improved it took less horse power and man power to operate them. The ploughman could now control the horses himself and over most of the country a pair of horses could do the work of the earlier, larger teams. (M.E.R.L)

maker. Ewart Evans in *The Farm and the Village*, 1969, talks to a saddler who had a rope walk at the back of his shop. The farms on the eastern side of Scotland nearly all had rope making tools called locally thrawcruicks, and which could twist together three and sometimes four strands of cord. With these the horsemen made their own ropes and plough lines. Hemp for rope making was originally grown in many parts of the country, but especially East Anglia.

Another innovation of the Middle Ages, the postillion riding one of the horses in a wagon team, has survived in one part of Britain— this time in Eastern Yorkshire and Lincolnshire. Mr. Cooper, saddler in Bridlington, remembers his father hiring out twenty to thirty of these wagon pads each year at 1/–d. per week during the harvest. They were used on the front horses of a team for a rider to control and drive them.

Basically there has been little change in the design of heavy horse harness in this country since the end of the Middle Ages. Very little information on heavy cart harness exists, but most of the more recent changes have been improvements to lighten and strengthen the harness. This was made possible by the increasing skill of the harness-makers and also the improved methods of manufacturing the harness furniture—buckles, chains and other fittings.

Chain traces replaced the rope ones, and metal fittings did much to increase the working life of a set of harness. So too did the use of waxed thread in place of leather thonging in the sewing together of the various pieces. Straps were made lighter and unnecessary expanses of leather, such as the 6 in to 8 in deep breeching straps and the enormous housings once worn, were reduced to a more workable size. Even as recently as the beginning of this century there were pleas from some harness-makers to 'turn out harness lighter, more comfortable and more pleasing to the eye' (*Saddlery and Harness*, 1902).

Good illustrations of heavy horses in harness before 1850 are difficult to find. This one comes from Stephen's Book of the Farm, and shows both shaft and trace harness from Mid-Scotland. Apart from some fancy stitching on the blinkers, the harness was not decorated. (M.E.R.L)

THE HEAVY HORSE HARNESS AS FINALLY DEVELOPED IN BRITAIN

Although many areas of the British Isles developed their own distinctive patterns of harness, basically they all conformed to the same recognisable outline. Three main types of harness are found, each designed for a different type of work; shaft work, trace work and ploughing.

For a set of shaft, or thiller, harness (Fig. 4), the following items are required: a bridle to guide the horse; a well fitting padded collar to take the hames and to which the short traces to the shafts are attached; a well padded cart saddle or pad, provided with a channel to take the back chain which holds up the shafts; a belly-band or wanty to stop the shafts from tipping up too far; and a set of breeching or britchen, which the horse uses to hold back the weight of the cart and if necessary stop it.

Trace harness (Fig. 5), or long gears, are used when horses are coupled one in front of the other, whether as help for the shaft horse to pull a laden cart or wagon, or when ploughing heavy land and walking in line down the furrow. The bridle, collar and hames are as for the shaft horse. The trace harness consists of a back-band to support the long trace chains, and a long crupper strap fixed at the collar, running the length of the horses back and ending in a

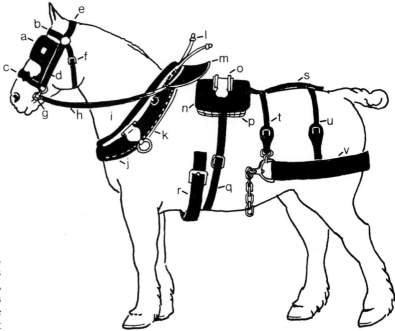

Fig 4
Modern shaft harness
of the London Pattern,
and a key to the names
of the parts of the
harness used in the text

Bridle	*Collar*	*Saddle*	*Breechings*
a blinker	i forewale	n saddle housing	s crupper
b brow band	j side-piece	o bridge	t loin strap
c nose band	k body (the	p pad	u hip strap
d cheek-strap	padding)	q girth strap	v breech band
e head-strap	l hames	r belly band	
f throat-lash	m housen		
g bit			
h bearing rein			

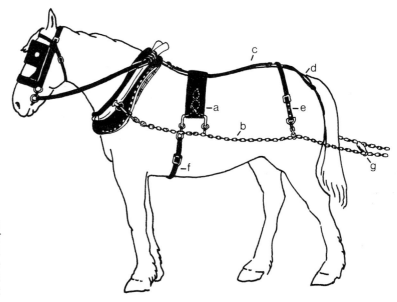

Fig 5
Modern trace harness of the Norfolk pattern and a key to the names of the parts of the harness used in the text

a	back band	e	hip strap
b	trace chains	f	belly band
c	crupper strap	g	spreader bar
d	dock		

dock round the horse's tail. The crupper strap keeps the back-band in position and usually supports hip straps which hang either side of the horse to take some of the weight of the traces and to avoid them getting under the horses feet when slack. A bellyband attached to the traces forward of the back-band prevents the more horizontal pull of the traces from pulling the collar up into the horse's windpipe. Trace harness was also used by the horses of the canal boatmen for pulling their craft.

Plough harness (Fig. 6), for working horses abreast, requires bridle, collar and hames, and a back-band to hold up the chains between the hames and the swingletree of the plough. Although many farmers use a crupper strap and hip-straps when ploughing abreast, on the whole only the plain plough band or back-band was used. No bellyband was needed as the downward pull of the traces kept the collar off the horse's windpipe. The name G.O. gears is used to describe plough harness over a large area of the Midlands. The origin of the term is the fact that in most of the Midland Counties when you talk to a horse and ask it to turn to the right, you call out 'Gee Oh'. As this is the direction the horses mostly have to turn on reaching the end of the furrow, the harness for

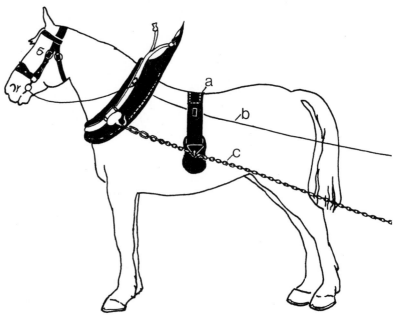

Fig 6
Modern plough harness
of the Scottish pattern

a plough band
b plough lines
c plough chains

working the horses in the plough became known as G.O. tack or gears.

These then are the different types of harness to be found about the country today. Through the years many improvements have been tried out to make them more efficient.

Inventors of improvements of saddlery and harness were amongst the first applications for protection of their ideas. Patent No. 31 was granted by Charles I in January 1625 to Ed. Knappe 'for his invention of an improved collar for horses whereby the animal is enabled to work with greater comfort'. Tens of thousands of patents were granted in subsequent years for ideas connected with the saddlery and harness trade. Every day brought fresh ideas, many of which were taken up by the trade and incorporated in the harness of the day, and many more which never left the drawing board.

A few examples of the more exotic failures are given below:

In the 1890s, a London evening paper announced that: 'a luminous harness for horses had been invented in order to avoid collision after dark'.

In 1893 an idea was patented for controlling horses by electricity. To start the horse a current was passed through terminals under the saddle, and to stop it, the current was passed through terminals in the nostrils of the unfortunate beast.

In 1910 a dung catcher was patented. This was a device fixed behind the horse like a deep tube under the tail and designed to catch the horse's dung—and presumably to keep it until passing the nearest midden!

But the final insult to the horse was the invention of a Frenchman who designed a vehicle which was driven in front from a seat, steered like a car and powered by a horse running in an enclosed frame just behind the driver. The accelerator pedal was fixed to a device which jabbed spurs into the horse's sides and the brake pedal brought a large disc up in front of the horse's face forcing it to stop!

Of the new ideas which were taken up by the harness trade, many were used nationally, but a lot more only found favour in limited areas in the same way that the various harness patterns found regional popularity. In the following chapters the regional variations will be described in more detail, and where possible the reasons for their local popularity given.

The harness trade was noted for the numbers of new ideas patented each year. One of the last for the heavy horse was the gas mask of the second World War. (M.E.R.L)

CHAPTER THREE

Bridles, Bits and Reins

OPEN v CLOSED BRIDLES

The main function of a bridle is to hold a bit in the horse's mouth, to which can be attached reins for the person controlling the horse to communicate to it which way he wants it to move. For the majority of heavy horse bridles there is also a second function; to provide a means of restricting the sight of the horse, usually to a narrow, forward and downward field of vision. It is this secondary function that gives us our main division in the patterns of heavy horse bridles used in Great Britain—open bridles without blinkers and closed bridles with them.

The arguments for and against the use of blinkers have been debated for the past 150 years. Societies were formed to promote their abolition, and many of the larger companies using heavy horses in the cities gave a lead. The Midland Railways Company's 3000 horses by the end of the last century were all wearing open bridles. Other railway companies followed suit, and Barclay and Perkins, one of the best known breweries of the day, also gave up their use. All these horses continued to work perfectly well without the use of blinkers, and yet the arguments for their retention won the day, for the majority of owners continue to blinker their horses right up to the present day.

What were the arguments in favour of limiting the horse's vision? The strongest one seems to have been that, by limiting the horse's vision, it only has to take note of what it sees ahead. It will not be troubled by unusual movements to the side and behind it, and thus will keep its attention on its work. If it has to stand for long hours in streets waiting while loading and unloading take place, it will be quieter and more docile if wearing blinkers.

Many argued that by limiting its vision, a horse is less likely to shy at strange objects or movements and to cause an accident, especially in the crowded streets of cities. This is the argument still used by those working heavy horses for delivery work amongst the noisy, bustling, fume-filled city streets of today. There were even arguments, in the past, for the retention of blinkers to protect the horse's eyes from the whips of their own drivers!

Judges at shows seemed to prefer to see harnessed horses wearing blinkers. Certainly in Scotland, competitors showing heavy horses in harness believe they would stand a poor chance of a prize if they brought a horse into the ring wearing an open bridle. Many people genuinely believed that the addition of blinkers to the bridle added to the smartness of the whole harness. The smarter the turnout required and the more expensive the harness, the more likely the bridle was to be blinkered.

The harness-makers too opposed any change towards simplicity. Many believed that by reducing the price of a bridle by the cost of the blinkers, they would reduce their meagre margins to unacceptable levels. It is interesting to note that during the height of the campaign to do away with blinkers, the Saddler's Trade Journal included in its pages a circular from one of the societies appealing to the trade to advocate their abolition to their customers. This was backed up by an editorial on the same subject and yet, for the next few months the journal ran articles on patterns of harness, all of which included blinkers on the bridles!

A pair of Suffolks at the Guinness Dairy Farms, Old Woking in Surrey, in the 1940's. Note the unusual use of both open and closed bridles on the same pair. The crocheted ear caps are worn to keep off the flies.
(M.E.R.L)

The abolitionists mustered just as many arguments against the retention of blinkers. As to the horses shying at unusual sights and movements, they maintained that if a horse is trained in an open bridle and has never had its vision limited, then it is less likely to be alarmed and run away if it can see what it could otherwise just sense and fear. The more distinctly a horse can see an object, the less likely it is to be frightened by it. That a few companies could use so many horses, for all kinds of work, without being blinkered, but with just as much safety and no greater trouble than blinkered ones, was a sufficient argument for the abolitionists to carry on the fight. Even under modern traffic conditions in cities, this has been proven by the Hull Brewery Co., who for many years have used horses wearing open bridles for delivery work in that city.

But they had other reasons to put forward. Many maintained that the horse's eyes stood a great chance of being injured by the draughts concentrated on them than by the carter's whip. Blinkers, they said, caused the head to heat and the cold draughts could cause the eyes to be damaged. The eyes were also subject to damage by physical contact with badly made and badly adjusted blinkers.

Neither could the abolitionists go along with the suggestion that blinkers added to the smartness of the horse. On the contrary, they believed that blinkers 'hid the most beautiful feature of a horse's head—the eyes'. Finally, they argued that by reducing the weight of the bridle by half, the horses were able to work more comfortably in a blinkerless bridle.

OPEN BRIDLE PATTERNS

Considering the fact that most young horses were trained to harness in some form of blinkerless bridle, it does seem strange that the use of the open bridle remained so limited, especially on the farms.

Even in parts of Scotland, where the open bridle was most commonly seen, young horses would often be trained in open bridles— 'an open yin lets them see roond aboot them', and later they would be converted to closed bridles 'tae stop them seeing ower much'.

But for the horsemen further north, living in bothies on farms working up to fifteen pairs of horses, to have to use 'blinders' on a horse was tantamount to not having the ability to handle them as any true horseman should. This north-eastern corner of Scotland was the stronghold of the open bridle where the men worked with the horses all day long cultivating the rich soil.

Further south in Fife and the Scottish Midlands, blinkers were preferred, but in southern Scotland the open bridle was again to be seen, especially around Lanarkshire and Peebles-shire, where at one time '90 per cent of the farmers in the district ploughed with horses wearing headstalls'. (A bit was attached to the headstall or manger-halter to turn it into a simple open bridle.)

One Glasgow harness-maker, as long ago as 1847, designed a set of harness which had removable blinkers. They were attached top and bottom by springs 'thus having a collar open or bridle closed as required'. The idea does not seem to have caught on.

South of the border the open bridle found few supporters amongst the farming communities, and most of those were in the Northern counties.

The simplest patterns of heavy horse bridle found in Great Britain are undoubtedly the open bridles found in many parts of Scotland, but particularly those found around Aberdeen and the rest of the north east. They consist (Fig. 7) of cheek-straps, head-strap and throat-lash, and either a light form of brow-band or a pair of ear-bands curving from the top of the head-strap round the front of the ears to the temple. Nose-bands are not normally

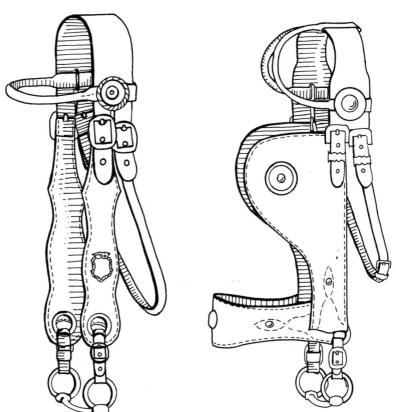

Fig 7 (left)
Scottish Open Bridle —
Aberdeenshire

Fig 8 (right)
Scottish Closed Bridle —
Fife

found in the northern form of these bridles, but in southern Scotland nose-bands are quite common, though the brow-band is sometimes discarded.

The whole construction of the bridle is very simple and light. The head-strap swells either side and divides in two to take the buckles of the cheek-straps and the throat-lash. As the brow-band is finished off with a loop either side, to attach it to the bridle, the head-strap is passed through the loop before buckling to the cheek-strap. Short bit-straps attach the bit to the bridle through reinforced holes in the leather at the bottom of the cheek-straps.

As whole buckles are normally used, keepers for the ends of the straps are seldom provided. It was often the practice to round the leather of the brow-band, ear-bands and throat-lash by rolling it round a piece of cord. This gave them the appearance of being flimsy, but in fact made them stronger. Some show bridles can be found with the leather on the cheek-straps and the nose-band also rounded, giving the complete bridle a skeleton appearance.

In its heaviest form, complete with the iron bit, this pattern of bridle weighed less than 3 lb, compared with the average of 6 lb for the blinkered bridle south of the border.

Open bridle patterns in England were on average 1 lb heavier than the Scottish pattern. As there was no tradition for open bridles, they were usually the same patterns as the blinkered ones, but without the blinkers. Indeed, many farmers first experimented with open bridles by cutting off the blinkers of an old bridle. The additional weight is mainly in the thickness of the leather, especially the substantial nose-band found on so many English bridles.

BLINKERED BRIDLES

Blinkered bridles then, were the rule over most of Britain and were found in many varied patterns. A few of the major variations will be described.

Once more, the lightest pattern of blinkered bridles is to be found in Scotland (Fig. 8). The cheek-strap and blinkers are usually cut in one piece, and occasionally both cheek-straps, blinkers and nose-band were cut from the one piece of leather. This avoided jointing the nose-band to the cheek-straps and gives a smoother and more comfortable fit for the horse. However, it was very extravagant with the amount of leather that was wasted.

What makes these bridles so much lighter than those used further south is the fact that they are only one thickness of leather. Only at the joints between the cheeks and the nose-band, and where the buckles are attached does one find double thicknesses of leather as reinforcement. Neither are the blinkers, or blinders as they are called in the north, blocked in any way to give added stiffening.

The basic construction is the same as the open bridle except for the addition of the blinkers. As with the open bridle, ear-bands are often worn in place of a brow-band. The bit is similarly attached by bit-straps, again often through a reinforced hole at the base of the cheek-strap.

The further south one travelled, the heavier the bridles became. In the north of England the Scottish pattern was used extensively, but double thicknesses of leather and the blocking of the blinkers were common. The practice of cutting the cheek-strap and blinker in one piece extends as far south as the Yorkshire bridle, which has a double cheek-strap sewn inside as a reinforcement. The Yorkshire bridle was usually made with a fixed head-strap and only one buckle, on the near-side, for adjustments (Fig. 9). This arrangement is also met with on the Cotswolds bridle where the bridle is known as a

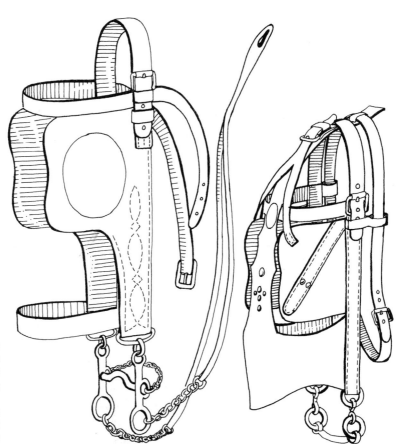

Fig 9 (left)
Yorkshire Bridle—with
curb bit and rein for
single line working

Fig 10 (right)
19th Century Full-Faced
Bridle—Herefordshire

mullin or mullen. The Cotswolds bridle is lighter than the Yorkshire bridle because the straps used were only $1\frac{1}{4}$ in wide compared with the $1\frac{1}{2}$ in and $1\frac{3}{4}$ in of the Yorkshire pattern. The thicknesses of straps make a lot of difference to the overall weight of a bridle.

Many areas have patterns of bridle that are light and robust using only the minimum thickness of leather to get the strength required. These bridles could weigh as little as 4 lb and give as much service as more elaborate designs. The farm bridles of East Anglia and the south-eastern counties are of light construction.

There was a constant cry from many quarters in the heavy horse world to make bridles lighter and thus more comfortable for the horse to wear.

The heaviest blinkered bridles were found in the Midlands and in many of the cities where it was more fashionable to dress the horses in elaborate harness. A typical Midlands bridle would weigh 7 lb complete with bit and brass decorations. Most of the added weight, however, comes from the double, and often as much as four thicknesses of leather that were used in their construction. The thicker and heavier the nose-bands became, the larger and thicker was the brace piece needed to support it to the cheek-strap.

In the London style bridle, the blinkers and brace piece were often cut from one piece of leather and sandwiched between double cheek-straps, resulting in a thickness of $\frac{1}{2}$ in of leather for the harness-maker to stitch through. It is little wonder that harness-makers in one area could find the cost of making a bridle double that in an area where a simple pattern was more acceptable.

THE FULL-FACED BRIDLE

This early pattern of blinkered bridle survives in only a few districts of England and Wales, chiefly in southern Cornwall and the Hereford, Radnor borders (Fig. 10). At one time it was more widely distributed in the southern part of Britain and is probably a survivor of the earliest form of blinkered bridle. There are examples of the pattern from the early eighteenth century in the Museum of Leathercraft at both Walsall and the Guildhall Museum in London.

The essential feature of the full-faced bridle is a broad piece of leather joining the top of the head-strap to the brow-band, and continuing down the front of the face to the nose-band. This gives a hooded effect on the horse wearing it, particularly as the nose-band tends to be thicker than normal. In its simplest form it is found with all but the head-strap cut out of one piece of very thick leather. Bridles of this pattern were made around Kington in Herefordshire until the last harness-maker closed shop. But they were not always liked by the wagoners. Bert Boulton, who has been with horses since he was ten, called them 'the owld fashioned bridles' and found them too heavy, as they tended to 'sweat a horse'. 'They were all right on a cold day.'

Around Penzance, where the pattern was being made by local saddler, Mr. Nicholls, until recently, the same argument was used against it by local farmers. It was too hot for the horse in summer. In southern Cornwall these bridles are used as a show bridle, the majority of farmers being content with a cheaper bridle without the full-face piece.

Another form of the full-face bridle was that worn by the pit

Clipping of the heavy horse in winter trace high allowed them to be more easily dried and cleaned and thus making chills less likely. This scene is from Cornwall where the full-faced bridle was a common pattern.
(M.E.R.L)

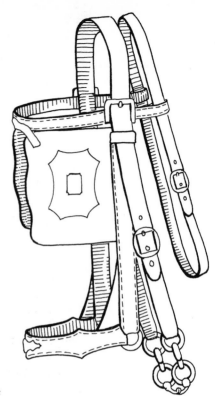

Fig 11 Loose cheeked Bridle—Shropshire

ponies. The piece between the top of the head-strap and the brow-band of these hooded bridles was designed to protect the pony's head from roof obstructions. The hooding of the eyes was also a protection against injury. Many of these 'ponies' were as big and strong as their relatives working on the farms above them in the sun and rain.

THE LOOSE CHEEKED BRIDLE

This bridle was a comparative latecomer to the harness scene and is a good example of an idea patented and taken up by the harness-makers within a fairly limited area. In April 1907, Mr. W. Owen of Mold in Flintshire patented a bridle which 'is constructed so that the strap carrying the bit is not connected to the nose-band'. Mr. Ryder, of Shrewsbury, who made many a loose-cheeked bridle in his day, described its main advantage (Fig. 11). 'The driver was working on the horse's mouth alone. With the fixed type there was a strain on the nose-band. You could get more leverage with a loose bitted bridle as all the pull was on the mouth.'

To keep the bridle in position a chin strap was fitted. This was an advantage when allowing a horse to graze or eat its 'bait' in the field. Most wagoners slipped the bit out of the horse's mouth to allow it to eat, and with the firm sided bridle there was always the danger of the horse rubbing its head and lifting the bridle up on to its forehead. This could not happen with the loose-cheeked bridle because the chin strap kept it in position whether the bit was in the horse's mouth or not.

The area in which the pattern was found included most of Shropshire, Cheshire, Flintshire and parts of Staffordshire and Lancashire. But, even within this area, its use was limited because it was a more costly bridle to produce than the firm sided one. They also tended to be on the heavy side, around the 7 lb mark, when brassed up and fitted with a bit.

BITS

Control of the horse through the bit should be possible with the least effort on the part of the driver. Careful training and the use of the correct bit can make this possible. The bits used for the heavy horse are almost invariably simple iron or steel snaffle bits which work on the corner of the horse's mouth. They are fitted to rest on the bars, or gums, of the mouth above the teeth and on the horse's tongue.

Various patterns of snaffle are used, depending on how responsive the horse is to the bit. The most comfortable bit used is the plain bent bit, known as the bucket-handle bit in many parts. Plain straight bits are also very common. Jointed bits were used more in the cities and can be more severe in use than the plain bar bits. Also less comfortable are the twisted bits made in the bent, straight and jointed patterns. They are used with horses that are hard mouthed —less responsive to the pull of the reins.

There were special patterns of bits produced for the Scottish market. The most commonly used was the knob end bit. Scottish patterns were fitted with rings so that they could be strapped to the bridle, making their removal for watering or feeding a simple matter.

Not all areas removed the bits for the horses to eat and drink, but in some parts the horsemen would never allow their animals to be fed with their bridles on. In these areas the bit would be a fixture on the bridle. But where the bits were habitually removed, a simple method of doing this was necessary. The most popular method was by means of a hook on one side of the bit and which was provided with a small drop ring to prevent it coming undone accidentally.

The link and tee methods of attaching the bit was most popular in East Kent and Sussex.

The curb bit was used mainly in towns and cities amongst the traffic. Like the snaffle, the curb bit rests on the bars of the mouth above the teeth, but the use of a curb chain gives it more power. The most commonly used pattern for the heavy horse is the Liverpool bit, whose designs allows different degrees of control depending on where the reins are attached.

A curb bit was also used in parts of Yorkshire and Lincolnshire. It was associated with working in a check rein (see p. 55). Mr. Fisher, a horseman from Holderness, comments: 'A heavy curb was found on most bridles associated with a check on the near side 'oss. I've never understood why! I've thrown many of these numb brutes away if I could find something else.'

The Yorkshire pattern has a low port, a U-shaped arch designed to press on the roof of the horse's mouth.

Other patterns of bit used in connection with the heavy horse include the mouthing bit. This is a straight snaffle provided with a small plate in the centre, to which a number of keys are attached. This bit is usually given to a young horse being bitted for the first time. The keys, being loose, move around and the horse plays with them and in doing so gets used to the idea of a bit in its mouth. Sometimes horses were provided with bits which had rollers, or cherries, along the length of the mouth-piece so that the horses could play with them whilst standing around for long periods during loading and unloading. For horses with very sensitive mouths bits with rubber mouth-pieces, or leather covered ones, were used. Wooden bits were also used until recently, for training horses.

But whatever the pattern of bit and whatever the type of horse, the bit must be the right size and adjusted properly in the horse's mouth. A properly bitted horse can be controlled without giving it any undue discomfort.

REINS

Different reins are used to control a horse in different ways. The driving reins convey to the horses, through the bit, the wishes of the wagoner or ploughman driving them. By his pulling on either rein, the trained horse knows whether it has to turn to the right or left, and if both are pulled together, to stop. A flick of the reins can be an indication for the horses to go forward. In most areas the use of reins is combined with the voice, the horse responding to either command. However, in parts of Scotland and Ireland voice commands were few and far between, so that the reins were the silent means of controlling the horses.

Reins for driving horses in carts and wagons are usually of leather, whilst those for ploughing, harrowing, etc. are invariably of rope, and called lines. When using lines it is normal practice to use a pair, one tied to the near-side bit ring of the near-side horse, and the other to the off-side ring of the off-side horse, and with some form of cross coupling between the horses, the simplest being a cord tied between the two bits.

The use of a single line to control the horses was common in parts of eastern England from southern Yorkshire to Cambridge. The 'Lincolnshire style' was to have a single line which split into two and fastened to each ring of the bit. Check reins, as they were called, could only be used on horses specially broken in to this type of driving. Where a pair of horses were working abreast, the check rein was attached to the near-side horse, and to the middle horse if three abreast. The horse was trained to come round to the left in response to a steady pull on the line. As the left hand section of the split rein was made shorter than the right hand one, a steady pull worked on the horse's mouth in much the same way as ordinary reins. To make the horse go to the right the driver gave the rein a few short 'checks' (jerks). A horse soon got used to this method of driving if coupled with words of command. Only slight pressure was needed to bring it to the left, and, on feeling a slight shake of

Ploughing with Percherons, three abreast, at the Chatteris ploughing match in 1953. The ploughman controls the horses with a single line to the nearside bit ring of the middle horse—a standard practice in that part of the country. (M.E.R.L)

the rein, to the right. Mr. Fisher found this method of driving 'ideal when the horses got used to it. But I'm afraid a few never would, and I lived on farms where they wouldn't allow the use of a check rein under any circumstances. Rough usage was sometimes evident, thus giving this method a rather bad name.'

Further south into Cambridgeshire the single line was not split like the check rein. It was attached to the near-side of the horse's bit only. As the horses here usually worked three abreast, the line horse was the middle one of the three. The signals were the same as those further north.

The horses not controlled by the check rein wore false lines. These were attached to the inside ring of the bit, brought behind the chin to the outside ring, then up through the rein ring on the hames and over the horse's back to the trace of the horse wearing the check rein. The false lines were simply to restrict the independent movement of the horses and keep them working together.

The bearing rein similarly is a rein designed to restrict the horse's movements. Used with the heavy horse it is attached to the bit rings and looped over the hames. Working in the fields it prevents the horse getting its head down to snatch a bite to eat as it works. They also help to keep a horse from turning its head, and presumably, as those who are in favour of blinkers argue, prevent the horse from being worried by what is going on behind him.

Some carters argued that a bearing rein also gave the horse some degree of support when it stumbled. Stephens, like many other writers refutes this, 'As to stumbling, he cannot recover himself with his head bound up—and the fall becomes worse.'

Reynolds, *Management and Breeding of Draught Horses*, 1876, puts forward further argument for their retention because of the use the horse makes of the bit for support when pulling a load, 'By using a properly adjusted bearing rein, a draught horse can, by using his intelligence, move a greater weight than if no bearing rein is used—because it gives support to the horse's head. A horse will use the bearing rein to support his head in a comfortable position.'

In spite of many such arguments for keeping the bearing rein, in the early part of the present century there was a determined movement to do away with them. Misuse of the bearing rein by even experienced horsemen led to great suffering for some horses. The Committee of the Cart Horse Parade held annually in London determined that 'no draught horse has any business with a bearing rein', and they made it a condition that any driver using one in the parade would be disqualified.

A rein with an entirely different function, which was often seen on horses at the above parade as well as on the roads, was the leading rein. The leading rein is used mainly when carting. One end is fastened through the near-side ring to the off-side ring of the bit with the other end usually buckled to the top of the crupper. Its purpose was to give the carter walking alongside his horses a quick means of controlling them should the need arise. As the carter or wagoner usually walks beside the shaft or thill horse, if the need arose, he could, by pulling on the lead rein, control the lead horse without having to go to its head.

In some areas the lead rein of the shaft horse goes back only as far as the saddle. Other areas wore lead reins on the off-side as well as the usual near-side rein, more for swank than utility.

HEMP HALTERS UNDER BRIDLES

The practice of wearing a light hemp halter under the bridle was common in many parts of England, but especially in Yorkshire and neighbouring counties. The idea could have originated in the army where it was common practice.

A young horse was often trained in one, it being possible to use the halter rope to tie back a restive one without the horse pulling

A pair of Shires at the Chatteris ploughing match in 1953, showing how the wearing of a halter under the bridle is utilized to tie back the furrow horse. Note, too, the Yorkshire pattern of hame hook. (M.E.R.L)

against the bit all the time and harming its mouth. Many horsemen found a halter rope very useful when bridling and unbridling a young horse.

But in Yorkshire and Lincolnshire particularly, the halter rope was necessary for their way of cross coupling horses working abreast, especially when worked with the single check rein. The halter rope was always coupled to the opposite horse's inside rein ring on the hame. If three horses were being worked, an extra halter rope was attached to the middle horse so that it was coupled to the horses on either side.

The halter was also worn under the bridle of some town horses. Here the argument for their use was that it was much safer to tie up a horse by its halter rope. If a horse were tied up by the reins, they argued, it stood a good chance of breaking the bridle.

But in parts of Lancashire, for your horse to be seen wearing a halter under its bridle, was an indication to all that your horse was for sale!

CHAPTER FOUR

Collars, Hames and Housens

The collar is a means of comfortably attaching a horse to its draught. Two types are in use on heavy draught horses, the breast collar and the neck collar.

THE BREAST COLLAR

The breast collar is a broad strap of leather, usually padded with felt, which goes round the breast of the horse so that its top almost touches the junction of the neck and shoulder. A strap over the neck keeps the collar in position. Draught hooks are attached at the shoulders to take the draught chains.

As we have seen, the breast collar preceded the neck collar, and although it fits the horse too low for a perfect pulling position, it is still used in many parts of the world, particularly in northern Europe. In those countries where the heaviest draught horses are found, neck collars have almost completely replaced the breast collar. Exceptions are found where a horse cannot wear a neck collar because of injury or shyness. Many horses would not have a collar put over their heads and as a result were worked in breast collars. So too were many young horses, it being found that breast collars in good condition were less likely to cause sores on the tender skin of their shoulders.

The movement of the breast collar across the breast can quickly cause a sore if a piece of dirt or grit is allowed to lodge between the collar and the horse. The strap over the neck too was often a cause of injury, and leather or metal shields were worn for this strap to ride on.

No one area of Britain used the breast collar more than any other. If a horse was only capable of working in one, then it was used as a last resort. However, for all but this few, the neck collar was the accepted form used on heavy horses.

THE NECK COLLAR

The neck collar is a ring of padding individually fitted to each horse so that it lies closely to the neck and shoulders but leaves clear the top of the neck in front of the withers and also the throat.

The roll, or forewale, of the collar consists of a tube of leather which is stuffed with straw until it is as stiff as a piece of wood. To this is attached the body, the padding of the collar, filled ideally with rye straw and covered with stout woollen collar cloth. The leather side pieces, or afterwale, cover the body to protect it from the weather and the wear of the draught hook and chains. The collar is padded in such a way that it is thickest where the wear is greatest, at the point of draught and where the trace chains must be kept away from the horse's sides. The shape of the padding also keeps the collar clear of the horse's throat and withers.

Unless the horse is fitted with a comfortable collar it is unable to work properly. Every horse should have its own collar, just as every horseman should have his own shoes. It should be easily placed on the shoulders. One that is too narrow and needs forcing on will cause injury. If it is too small it is liable to choke the horse. On the other hand, a collar that is too large and moves about when the horse is pulling, can cause even greater injuries. For this reason, the fit of the collar is of more importance than any other part of the heavy horse's harness.

A collar of the correct size but badly shaped is made to fit a horse by soaking it in water overnight. Next day it is put on the horse and drawn to the shape required by the hame straps and the horse lightly worked during the day. This adjusts the collar to all the peculiar inequalities of the shoulder and neck of the horse.

The practice of wagoners knocking collars on the floor of the stable to widen them, so that they would fit over the horse's head easier would not only spoil the collar, but cause discomfort to the horse.

Because a horse's neck is thicker at the bottom than the top, the collar is correspondingly wider at the bottom. But as the crown of a horse's head is broader than his muzzle, the collar has to be put on over his head upside-down and turned round when on the neck. If the wagoner had gone to all the trouble of plaiting and braiding the horse's mane before putting on the collar, he had to be sure to 'swizzle' it in an anti-clockwise direction or the mane would be ruffled and all his good work undone. Many horses, particularly the Suffolks, with small heads and large necks, could have their collars put on the right way up.

Many ideas were patented for instruments to measure a horse's neck for fitting a collar. Collars themselves are measured inside the forewale from top to bottom and measurement must be as accurate as possible, not hit and miss as described in *Saddlery and Harness* in 1902:

'If a collar fits properly, the saddler's peace of mind is assured. If it is a little too tight, his thoughts revert to that black bogey of a collar maker to whom tradition assigns the possession of a rule with one thick and one thin end. If the collar is bare measure, he thrusts the thin end well up into the cap and if too full puts in the thick end so making the measurement correct one way or the other. This bit of artfulness serves no purpose when the collar is on the horse's neck.'

Possibly the largest collar ever fitted to a horse was the one made by John Angus & Co. of Glasgow in 1907, measuring $33\frac{1}{2}$ in long and 15 in wide. Another of 33 in is at present on display at the 'Charlie Butler' pub in Mortlake, London, and was made for a champion shire gelding, Bower King John, who stood 18·2 hands. Stallions brought into harness after being at stud usually needed very large collars, but these would have to be changed for smaller ones as they worked off some of their surplus weight.

PIPE COLLARS

Some horses choke easily and need to wear a pipe, or windpipe, collar to keep the pressure off the lower windpipe (Fig. 12). Mr. Danscombe of Oakford, Devon now seventy years old, remembers

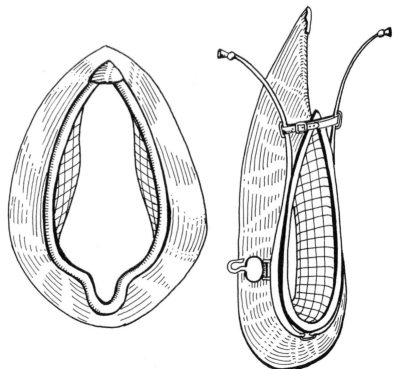

Fig 12 (left)
Piped Collar—to prevent a horse choking

Fig 13 (right)
Scottish peaked collar—with wide hames to match

how easily a horse could choke: 'Some horses will hold a load in the collar until they choke. I seed it once. The boss went back to fetch a horse with crippins (trace harness) to give a horse with a big load of mangolds a pull out. The horse was holding the load from falling back down the bank and into the river. By the time the boss had returned, the horse had chocked and went down, and the load of mangolds went into the river.'

If the horse had been wearing a pipe collar he would not have choked, because the forewale is shaped to take pressure off the windpipe. The pipe shape is kept by fixing a metal piece into the forewale during the stuffing operation.

Many people use a pipe collar on a colt when breaking it into harness, to prevent it choking itself during its energetic rushes for freedom. But the horses most prone to choking were those with long sloping shoulders and fine withers. As the Clydesdale breed have less oblique shoulders than the other breeds, this may be the reason why pipe collars were almost unknown north of the border. It could be that the design of the padding of the Scottish collar made a pipe unnecessary. The padding was often quilted at the bottom and this kept the pressure away from the windpipe.

THE SCOTTISH PEAKED COLLAR

The Scottish Peaked Collar, or brecham, has many admirers both in this country and abroad, particularly America (Fig. 13). It was used chiefly as a show collar as the added expense of a peak contributed nothing to its quality from the work point of view. It was developed in the middle of the last century from the form of collar used in the Lothians (Fig. 14). This collar had the side pieces and housen, or cape, stiffened with strips of whalebone and made in one piece. The broad cape became narrower and taller until it lost its function as a protection for the collar body, and finished up as pure decoration.

The Scots are very proud of their brechams, or long tops, but south of the border they came in for a lot of good humoured criticism. One English saddler described them as 'church steeples'. Another writes, 'I have seen these collars as though they were cast in a mould and from the point of view of workmanship leave nothing to be desired; but down south they are decidedly out of place and nobody wants one.' He goes on to describe how a Scottish estate owner in the south introduced them to his southern carters, but the men refused to use them and they had to be discarded when still almost new. The men could not face the taunting they received from their fellow carters and they would rather leave the estate than use the high top collars.

The peaked collars were heavy collars compared to those further south and this prompted one southern saddler to write: 'Can anyone justify the hanging of 20–30 lb and the weight of the hames (11 lb) on the neck of a horse when a collar of 12 to 14 lb will do as well? I have just made a 23 in collar weighing $14\frac{3}{4}$ lb, and I am prepared to bet my oldest boots that it will stand more rough usage than the awful looking thing the high top collar turns into in its old age.'

Mr. Smith, saddler at Biggar, is a great supporter of the peaked collar, 'A good collar should come to a point in two straight lines from the widest part. The inside too should come to a point in a similar way.' He believes that only a Scottish collar-maker could make the body which the Scottish saddlers turned into the impressive high tops so proudly displayed in the Scottish show rings and at ploughing matches.

Not all Scottish collars had peaks on. Most of the working collars had none, and the quality of workmanship and materials used were

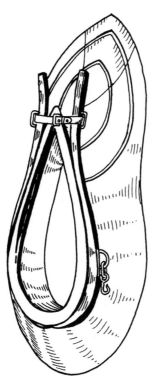
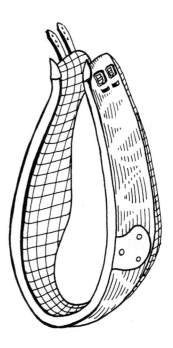

Fig 14 (left) Lothian Collar—c.1825 —showing the development from the detached housen to the peaked collar

Fig 15 (right) Open Collar

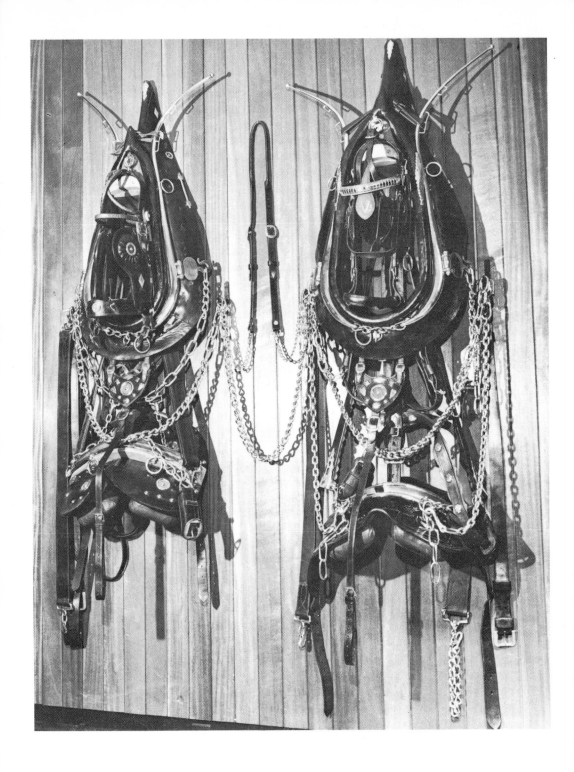

still first class, but they were still a heavy collar. One Scottish saddler was moved to comment, 'There must be a lot of collars approaching 30 lb as there is lining upon lining in them; to reduce this weight would improve the horse's comfort.'

Peaked collars were made as far south as Newcastle, but the typical collar of this area has a cape on top much in the shape of the old lothian collar. The only other part of Great Britain where collars with side-pieces and housens all in one piece were found was south Wales, and here the collars were much lighter.

The lightest of the heavy horse collars were found in the south and east of England. The Norfolk pattern was one of the lightest. The leather side-pieces were cut very narrow towards the top, exposing to view the cloth lining of the body. In the Kent pattern the body lining showed all round, so narrow were the side-pieces. Though most of the heavy horse collars manufactured in Walsall were on the lighter side, the local harness-makers in the Midlands tended to make a much heavier collar, weighing from 20 to 30 lb.

If appearance alone were the determining factor for the comfort of a collar on a horse, then the Scottish collars take top place, but as weight is probably of more significance, the collars of the south are to be preferred by the horses themselves.

OPEN TOP COLLARS

The open top, or split, collar (Fig. 15) was designed to part sufficiently to slip on to a horse's neck without having to go over its head. As with breast collars they were used in small numbers all over Britain for horses that would not allow a collar to go over their heads. There were horses too which were possessed with large heads and small necks so that the only way they could be fitted with a collar was by using an open top. It is generally felt that they are inferior to the rigid neck collar, because, the more solid the collar, the less likely a horse is to get sore shoulders.

Two sets of shaft harness in the harness room of Vaux brewery, Sunderland, where sixteen Percherons are used to deliver beer. The peaked collars are by Jobson and Sons of Alnwick and are more usually associated with Scotland.
(*Guiness Time*)

To keep a split collar as rigid as possible, extra reinforcement was built into the throat, and when being opened to put on a horse it should be parted only enough to pass over the horse's neck. Every time it is forced open wider than is necessary it loses some of its rigidity. The straps at the top, usually two in number, were made to buckle the collar together as firmly as possible, but even so there is often movement between the split, and to avoid chafing the horse's withers a zinc, or vulcanite, shield is fitted between the neck and the collar top.

Because one always stands on the near side of a horse when

putting the collar on, the buckles on the open top were placed on the near side.

Whether or not the heavy horses in the south-west of England and in the whole of Ireland, had oversized heads compared with the rest of the British Isles is a matter for some conjecture, but in these areas the open top collar was the normal collar in use on all heavy horses. In spite of the advantages of the rigid neck collar, tradition demanded that open tops should be used, and the only argument heard favouring their use was that 'no horse likes to have a collar passed over its head'.

OTHER PATENT COLLARS

Many patent ideas were tried out to improve collars. One of the most commonly used was the 'patent elastic steel horse collar'. Its advantages were described in a trade magazine in the 1890s: 'These collars cure sore shoulders and prevent them in future. They are invaluable for horses with tender skins enabling them to work with comfort, where, with ordinary collars they would be continually under treatment for galls.'

Many wagoners used these collars whenever a horse developed sore shoulders. One would be found in most stables, kept for this purpose. In Herefordshire they were used regularly in the hopfields, especially when the hop binds had grown, and working between the rows was a hot and sticky job. The metal collar kept the shoulders cool. The Kent growers, however, preferred to keep to the ordinary padded collar.

Pneumatic collars, in which air took the place of stuffing, appeared on the scene at the turn of the century, but never achieved much popularity, except in parts of southern Scotland around Galloway. James Muir, who farmed in that area, found them better for the horses. Nearly all the collars used by his neighbours at the end of the heavy horse era, were of this type. They seldom burst, but if they did a repair kit was kept handy to mend them. Away from this area most people who tried them found them unsatisfactory for one reason or another. The usual criticism levelled against them was that 'they made the horse sweat and blister at the shoulders'.

As most horsemen are very conservative in their ways, many new ideas were dismissed even before they were given a proper trial. Collars like the one described below seldom reached the production stage. 'Loveday and Sons of Islip produced a collar in 1891 consisting of a row of spiral springs, so placed as to give to every movement of the horse's muscles, enabling him to utilise his whole strength without hurting him. They never pinch or give sore shoulders, and will last much longer than any ordinary collar.'

Even attempts at improving the stuffing of a collar were doomed to failure. The Sanitary horse collar with stuffing consisting of granulated cork, 'which never gets hard, but is cool and elastic on the horse', was also fitted with removable linings which could be washed. The idea never caught on even though it was advertised as 'the greatest boon ever introduced for the relief of cart and other hard working horses'.

In spite of all the efforts to improve horse collars, those in use today are of the old and well tried patterns of the past. In the minds of horsemen no satisfactory alternative has been found to the collar made with leather and stuffed with straw.

HOUSENS

The *Farmers' Dictionary*, c.1840, advocates that collars, 'require to be surmounted with such a cape as shall prevent rain from getting between the cushion and the shoulder, there to heat, irritate and even to blister the skin'.

Still known as a cape in many parts of the country, the housen had a useful, protective function. At its most practical development, especially in the southern parts of the British Isles, it consisted of a stiffened, rectangular piece of leather measuring approximately 12 in by 24 in (Fig. 16). It was attached to the hames in such a way that in fine weather it stood upright, and in wet conditions was dropped to lie flat and cover the area between the collar and the saddle. Most horsemen only attached these housens during the winter months, or other times of wet weather. The housen was

Fig 16 (left)
The southern form of housen—attached to the hames in the upright position. The top strap was released to lay the housen flat between the collar and the saddle

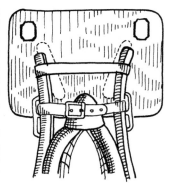

Fig 17 (right)
Large conical housen, stiffened with canes and fixed to the collar—West Midlands, nineteenth-century

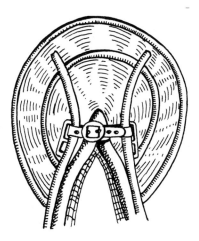

raised again from the dropped position after the rain finished, because, if left down, it tended to heat the horse about the shoulders. By raising it, air could circulate more freely about the horse's withers.

This type is still in use in southern England today, but over most of the rest of the British Isles the housen has degenerated into a small crescent shaped decoration for the top of the collar, or has even disappeared from the harness altogether.

In the first half of the nineteenth century some parts of the country attached large sheets of leather to the back of the collar. A painting, c. 1820, by Thomas Weaver (opposite) shows a pair of horses yoked to the plough and carrying huge sheets of leather in the upright position, rather reminiscent of a yacht carrying full sail. It is difficult to imagine what advantage was to be gained by raising this enormous housen in such a fashion, after the rain, rather than removing it altogether. To quote the *Farmers' Dictionary* again: 'A large, erect, spreading collar-cape, very common in many parts of England, is a very absurd appendage, principally to catch the wind, and in consequence, somewhat to embarrass the action or neutralise the power of the horse.'

The crescent shaped housen found in the Midlands was at first a sizable fixture on top of the collar (Fig. 17). It was large enough to provide protection from the rain driving from the front or even falling straight down. But it was of little use if the rain were driving in the same direction as the horses were moving. It was usually shaped by sewing canes into the rim of the housen, covering with leather and stitching both sides. They were attached to the collar with leather thonging. Later versions of this crescent housen were smaller and eventually they were merely convenient pieces of leather to decorate with brass ovals or octagons.

In parts of Wales, northern England and Scotland, the housen developed into a peak on top of the collar and which was part of the collar itself. The housen and side-pieces of the collar were cut in one and stiffened with canes. According to Hasluck in *Harness Making*, 'this involves a great waste of leather and is unnecessary'. On the question of the need for a housen of any sort, Hasluck says, 'Experience has demonstrated that neither the horse nor the collar is any the worse without such a device.' This opinion seems to be borne out by all but the southern counties of England. In the south the housen still has a function to perform whilst elsewhere it remains a pure decoration.

In Norfolk, where the housen is known as a fan, to 'put ones fan on' meant one was dressing up the horse for a trip to town. Likewise, most of the Midland wagoners spoken to regarded the small

Part of the painting by Thos. Weaver, showing the large housens worn in some areas in the early nineteenth century. The horses are harnessed in tandem and the one nearest the plough wears a saddle with an iron 'bend', still used in that part of Shropshire till the end of the horse era. (*Radio Times Hulton*)

crescent housens of the area as 'fancy pieces to finish off the collar', and knew of no other purpose for their presence there.

Though there are still devotees of the housen to this day, one cannot help agreeing with Hasluck that the collar and horse are none the worse without them, especially when one realises that the areas where they were most used are amongst the driest in the country, and the areas where they have disappeared altogether, amongst the wettest. If they had not had some attraction as a means of decorating the collar, it is doubtful if they would have survived in any but a few of the southern counties.

HAMES

The hames form a rigid frame round the neck collar and, being fitted with a means of attachment, enable a horse to be coupled to its draught.

Originally all hames were made of wood and in many parts of Britain wooden hames were used up to the end of the heavy horse era. The earliest method of attaching a horse to its draught was by use of rope traces tied through a hole in the hames. This is probably the method employed in the illustration from the Luttrell Psalter (Fig. 3) and can still be seen in use today in parts of eastern Kent. Later, iron hooks were fitted to the wooden hames and chains replaced ropes as traces in all but a few areas. The wooden hames would be cut out by the wheelwright, usually from ash or beech, and passed to the blacksmith, who made the iron fittings, either plain hooks for taking the links of the trace chains or staples to take the 'T' fitting popular in some parts.

Wooden hames were usually painted, traditionally red or blue, to help preserve the wood. In Scotland, where a less bulky pattern was used for ploughing, the wood was varnished.

To get a less bulky hame, iron was used in the form of a casing or as strengthening straps round a thinner wooden hame. Iron cased hames were stronger and lasted longer. They replaced the wooden ones for most farm and town work by the turn of the century. All steel hames were the final development, with brass and nickel cased ones used for decorative purposes.

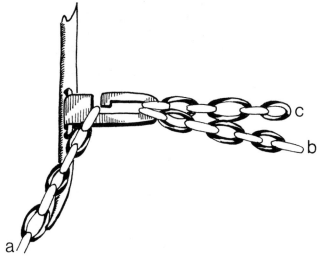

Fig 18
The Yorkshire pattern of hame hook—and the method of Attaching; a, the pole chain, b, the trace chain, and c, the britchen chain

Once iron cased hames began to be used, factories took over from the local craftsmen in their manufacture. But standardisation was slow to come because of the number of local patterns, some of which were determined by the local methods of harnessing. Typical of this was the Yorkshire pattern of hame, used in those areas of Yorkshire and Lincolnshire where wagons were fitted with poles instead of shafts. Here the hame hook was used, not only for the draught chains but also to attach both the britchen chain and the short chain to the front of the pole, used when the horses were backing the wagon (Fig. 18). To prevent the chains jumping off the hook when backing, a square face was necessary on the front of the hook. In later years a separate hook was provided below the draught hook to take the pole chain.

Short hames were made especially for work in orchards, to avoid catching the tops in the low branches. Some ploughmen preferred short hames with blunt tops for working horses abreast. This minimised the possibility of one horse injuring another when tossing its head about. Some hames had large round knobs fixed to the top for this reason. In a similar fashion knobs were once attached to the horns of oxen. In other areas carters liked the long hames so that they could run the reins between them, instead of using rein rings.

In Scotland, to compliment the peak of the high top collar, extra long hames with a wide outward sweep were the fashion. The Scots also had their own pattern of draught hook.

Although the majority of hames were fitted with plain draught hooks to be used for all purposes about the farm, there were also hames manufactured with fittings specially designed for one type of job. Shaft hames were fitted with fixed draught chains and could only be used for a horse working in shafts. Similarly, body hames were specially made for the body, or middle, horse in a team working in line. These hames had a short chain ending in a hook which could be attached to the draught chains running from the front horse, or leader, back to the wagon or plough.

Shifting draught hames were mentioned in an earlier chapter (p. 32). They were designed so that the draught hook could be raised or lowered in such a way that whatever the height of the point of resistance of the load the horse was pulling, a suitable adjustment to the height of the hame hook could be made, to find the best point from which the horse could pull (Fig. 19). Although shifting draught hames were used in small quantities over most of Britain, it was only in the West Country that they were used extensively. Even in the areas where they were most found, and

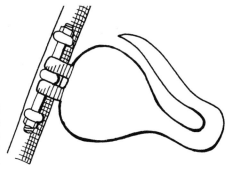

Fig 19
Shifting draught hame hook—shown here in the middle of three positions to which it can be set

although most of the wagoners knew their purpose, few in fact ever bothered to alter them to suit the work being done.

The idea of shifting draught hooks was used as long ago as 1847 by a Scottish harness-maker. In that year a set of harness fitted with a hook that could be raised or lowered, by re-arranging a number of washers, won a prize at the Edinburgh Agricultural Show.

The local nature of their use is emphasised by the fact that few Walsall manufacturers included shifting draught hames in their catalogues, and most of those produced were made by a Bristol firm.

In Norfolk, and a few other places, the hames were lashed together, both top and bottom, by leather thonging. In all other areas the tops were kept together by a strap, but there was considerable variation in the method of attaching the hames at the bottom. The most common method was a simple chain and hook, which could only be released after the top strap had been undone.

Many horsemen insisted on having a method of quickly releasing the hames in the event of a horse choking or going down between the shafts. Once the hames are released the pressure is taken off the collar and the chances of the horse choking are considerably lessened. The quickest way to release the hames attached by chain and hook at the bottom was to cut the top hame strap. Many sets of hames were furnished with dog tackle, a quick release hook, which made unnecessary the cutting of the top strap. The skid tackle used on some of the wooden hames in the south east had a similar function. But, particularly north of the border, there were many horsemen who would only allow their hames to be fastened at the bottom by a strap, which was not only easier for every day releasing the hames, but in emergency could be cut to free the horse.

The country was equally divided as to whether it was necessary to remove the hames from the collar each time or if they should be left on. Those for removing hames argued that, not only did it make the collar much lighter, but also allowed it to expand before being taken off over the horse's head. Hames left on the collar also tend to 'rust' the leather and so spoil the collar. Those who argue for leaving the hames on the collar point out that, by removing the hames, the collar changes its shape and only by keeping the hames on is the horse saved from suffering with sore shoulders. A number of patents were filed for collars with permanently attached hames, and such a pattern was extensively used in Australia.

The fit of the hames on the collar is almost as important as the fit of the collar on the horse. If they are not properly tightened close to the collar, whilst pulling a load in wet weather the collar will tend to get out of shape and cause the horse galled shoulders.

MEETER STRAPS

Sometimes spelt meter or metre straps, they attach the collar and hames to the saddle. They keep the collar from pitching forward on to the horse's neck when it puts its head down. Because bearing reins run from the bit round the hames, they become ineffective if no meeter straps are worn to keep the collar attached to the saddle.

The Midland's way of attaching the collar was by fixing two short straps to the top of the collar and these buckled to corresponding straps on the saddle. There is an old saying in south Shropshire that if one meeter strap is seen undone it must be an untidy wagoner, but if both are left undone then the culprit is an untidy farmer!

In Scotland meeter straps were seldom worn, and where they are found they are attached by a spring hook to a small metal dee sewn under the top of the collar. In Yorkshire and neighbouring counties the meeter strap was usually looped over one of the hames or through the rein rings on the hames. In south-eastern England the meeter strap was looped over the top hame strap. Norfolk collars had a crupper loop, a loop of leather sewn on to the top of the collar. The meeter strap was attached to the tree of the saddle and doubled back through the crupper loop.

In fact there were as many ways of attaching the collar to the saddle as there were saddle patterns throughout the country.

CHAPTER FIVE

Saddles and Breechings

CART SADDLES

The cart saddle consists of a pad, also called a panel, attached to a wooden frame, called a tree, and this in turn is usually covered by a leather housing (Fig. 20). The bridge of the tree is provided with channel, or trough, and into this fits the back chain, or ridger, which is usually fixed to the shafts. A girth strap passes under the belly of the horse to keep the saddle in position.

The purpose of the saddle in heavy horse harness is to take a small part of the weight of a shafted vehicle, especially two wheeled carts. By taking a small proportion of the weight—a tenth or twelfth of the weight of the cart—the vehicle is balanced, and a correctly balanced load takes a lot less energy for the horse to move it than one that is badly balanced. As a four-wheeled wagon carries all its own weight, where shafts are used, the saddle merely takes the weight of the shafts. Going up a steep hill with a loaded cart, a horse is helped by placing a little more of the weight of the cart on to its back. Doing this gives the horse a better grip. The carters often added the weight by standing on the shafts of the cart but this was not regarded as good horsemanship. The weight put on to the saddle is best altered by making the back chain shorter or longer. The longer it is, the lower the shafts and the more the weight of the load is thrown on to the horse's back. For this reason carts were favoured to wagons in hilly districts and areas where the going was soft.

In order to take this extra weight on its back it is very important that the horse is fitted with a well padded and well fitted saddle. The first rule in the fitting of a saddle is that it should bear on the back and ribs and not on the spine or withers, which will not stand pressure. The pad should be big enough to give an equal bearing over an area suitable to the weight being placed on the back. Hasluck recommends that the pad be thicker in the front than at the back so that it will not sink down and press on the shoulder bone under a load. A cart saddle that is too narrow may cause the withers to be pinched, causing fistulous withers, especially as the weight is thrown forward when going down hill in a heavily loaded cart.

The width of a saddle is determined by the size of saddle tree ordered. There are two possible measurements for a cart saddle tree. One is the length of the boards to which the padding is attached, and the other is the distance across the tree between the outside edges of each board. There was long correspondence between saddlers in their trade journal as to which was the correct way to measure a tree, and it would appear that the majority of them ordered trees according to the length of the boards. Those who measured across the tree were in the minority and each side vowed that their

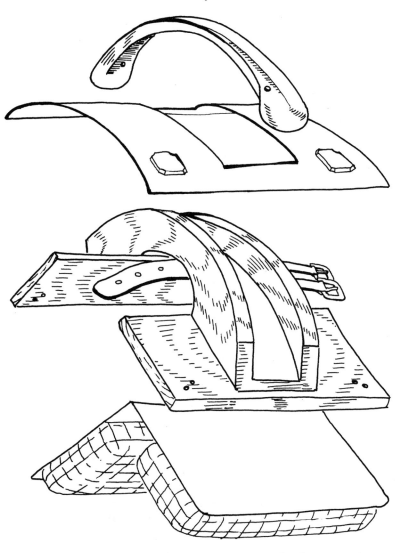

Fig 20
Exploded view of saddle

reading from top to bottom
metal channel for the back chain, leather housing, saddle tree complete with straps for attaching to the crupper strap and the collar, and the pad, or panel

method was the only sensible way. As it is important that the back chain should be kept well away from the horse's sides, it is necessary to use a tree that is wide enough to do this. According to Hasluck, the measurement should be taken across the tree, and if the boards are too long they should be cut, equally back and front, to about 12 in overall. However, as most trees were made with upward curving fronts to the boards, to cut these in any way would be a waste, so the ideal would seem to be to order a tree whatever measurement was wanted across its width and to specify the length of the boards required.

The trees are made from elm or beech. They have to be strong, but no heavier than is necessary. Beech is particularly easy to carve and resistant to wear and stresses in all directions. Many saddlers preferred elm, and some smoked them 'in exactly the same way as though they were sides of bacon hung in a drying house'.

At one time saddle trees were made locally to the saddler's own design, but as the specialist manufacturers took over, designs were standardised to about a dozen patterns. Apart from the tree for the Scottish saddle, they all followed the same basic shape—two boards fixed either side of a grooved arch. The pattern chosen depended on whether the local preference was for the leather housing to be nailed to the top of the bridge, to a step half-way down the side of the bridge, or to the boards themselves.

The simplest, but certainly not the most beautiful, cart saddle is that found in parts of East Anglia and the south-eastern corner of Kent and Sussex. It consists of a tree with a well padded panel tied to the boards with leather thongs. They are usually worn without a leather housing of any description, though decorated housings were often kept separately to be worn only when going into town, or occasionally the head carter had one on his saddle as an indication of his rank. Saddlers in the area argued that a leather housing served no real purpose, and as saddle trees are often broken, they are inexpensive to replace if left uncovered. Outsiders argued that they presented a crude and primitive appearance, and that 'tops should be added to save the pad back and to preserve the packing from hardness by exposure'. No metal channels or protective plates were fixed to these saddles, and in south-eastern England, to keep the back chain from chafing the sides of the horse, a specially shaped bar of iron, known as a ridger iron or yoke, is used. At either end of the ridger iron short lengths of chain was fixed so that the shafts, or rods, can be attached (Fig. 21).

A similar type of iron was used in south Shropshire and Hereford-shire. Known locally as a bend, it was used with a saddle on the horse nearest the plough when ploughing in line with a team of

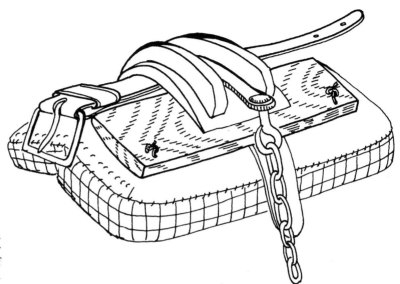

Fig 21
Kentish Saddle—with
no housing. A 'redger
bar' was used in place of
a back chain

three or more. Apart from these special fixtures, over the whole of Britain the back chain is normally found attached to the shafts of the carts, with one notable exception. The canny Cornishman worked out that it was better economics to keep one back chain for every saddle than one on every set of shafts on the premises. So the saddle in those parts is usually found with a back chain strapped loosely into place in the trough.

The standard London and Walsall patterns of saddle use a tree with a stepped groove so that the leather housing can be fixed below the top of the trough. Metal channels are fitted to take the wear of the back chain and as an added precaution, to protect the horse's sides leather flaps about 7 in to 9 in deep are often nailed to the boards of the tree.

The girth strap is also nailed to the boards, sometimes only a single one, and sometimes two. Walsall and the Midlands generally favoured the double girth. A double girth was said to be necessary in hilly areas to keep the saddle in its proper place. If only one girth is worn, when going downhill the saddle is often tipped up by the forward thrust of the back chain against the front face of the channel. With a double girth this cannot happen. It was also strongly argued that a second girth was a good form of insurance against the danger of one girth breaking when the horse was in a heavy pull. There is a practice in the Midlands of crossing the girths under the belly of the horse 'to stop the saddle slipping back'. The girth strap was always made to buckle on the near side of the horse.

The Lancashire, or Liverpool pattern of saddle invariably has double girths (Fig. 22). The saddle is a narrow one with the housings nailed on to the top of the wooden trough. With deep side flaps of 9 in to 12 in the saddle has the appearance of sitting very high on the horse's back. A slight rise, or chine, is built into the front housing of the saddle to keep it clear of the horse's withers. Further south, where a similar pattern of saddle was made, the more usual practice was to cut away a small portion of the housing at this point. Housings were nailed to the top of the tree down through Shropshire and the Welsh border counties.

Over most of the other counties of England, the practice was to nail the housing half-way up the trough of the tree, except in Yorkshire and Lincolnshire where the housing was nailed flat on to the boards (Fig. 23). The lining of the panel was then sown on to the saddle through the leather of the housing before being stuffed. Very short saves, or flaps, were nailed to the boards. The fore housing of the Yorkshire saddle was given a definite chine, and the further north one travels, the higher the chine becomes. The Yorkshire harness-makers achieved the chine on the front housing by cutting the back edge of the housing in a shallow V. The deeper the angle, the higher the chine in front.

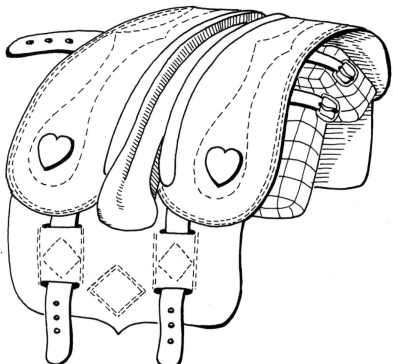

Fig 22
Liverpool-style saddle—
with the housing nailed
to the top of the bridge

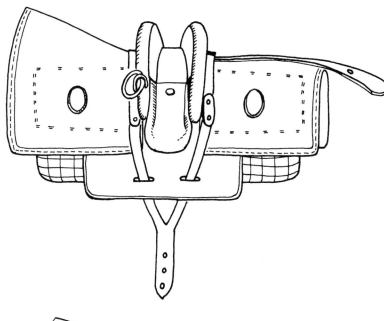

Fig 23
Yorkshire/Lincs-style
saddle. Housings nailed
direct on to the boards of
the tree and the pad
sewn direct on to the
leather housing

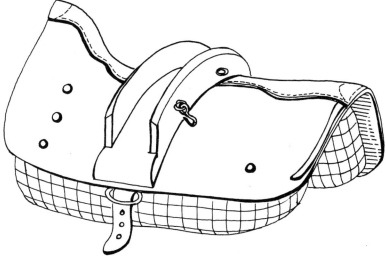

Fig 24
Scottish saddle—with
high chine to keep the
withers from touching
the housing. The
breechings are attached
by hooks to the bridge
of the saddle

The chine on the front of the Scottish saddle is greater than that of any other regional pattern (Fig. 24). The high withers of the Clydesdale dictated this. If a chine of a similar height were made for a saddle of one of the English breeds, it would get in the way of the top of the collar. As the Clydesdale has less oblique shoulders than the other breeds, plus the fact that the Scottish collar was padded differently, the sit of the collar is more upright and does

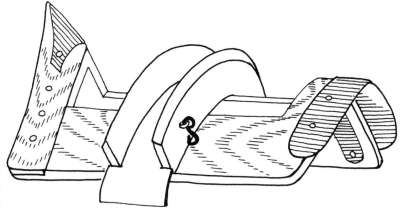

Fig 25
The tree of a Scottish
saddle—showing the
specially built up front

not interfere with the high chine of the saddle. A special tree was used for making these Scottish saddles (Fig. 25).

In the making of a Scottish saddle, the housings are cut along the length of the saddle instead of the breadth. They are lined to give them added strength, and after removing the bridge or crub, of the tree, the two covers are tacked to the tree separately, and pulled together at the top with stout wax thread. Next, the top joint is covered with two strips of leather, or bars. The bridge is then replaced on top of the housing and nailed firmly back on to the boards, and a metal channel fitted into the groove. At this point the padding is done and lined either with collar check or basil. The method of attaching the single girth is by doubling it through a civet ring attached to the wooden tree.

Where a pair of horses are attached to a vehicle either side of a central pole, as is the way with most of the brewery drays, there is no weight to be taken on the horse's back, so a very lightweight saddle, known as a pad, is used.

BREECHINGS

Horses harnessed to a central pole are coupled to the front of the pole by chains to the bottom of the hames. The collars, being attached to the rest of the harness, cannot move forward, so that when reversing the dray, they take the weight on the front chains.

When reversing a shafted vehicle, however, the horse is supplied with more substantial breechings which it can push against. They fit round the horse's breech and are attached to the shafts so that, as the horse 'sits' into them, the vehicle is reversed or prevented from overtaking the horse when going down a steep hill.

The breech band is supported by hip and loin straps attached to a crupper on top of the horse's rump. The word crupper is confusing, when applied to the heavy horse harness. For riding and light driving harness, the crupper is attached to the saddle and has a loop at the end which passes under the horse's tail and prevents the saddle from moving forward. On heavy horse breechings the crupper is seldom provided with such a loop, or dock. It is probable that the wearing of a dock under the tail was more popular in the past. All the drawings of horses in harness at the beginning of the nineteenth century show them wearing docks. The breechings on the harness in Newton's catalogue of 1872 are also provided with one, but later catalogues show only a small loop provided for hanging up the breechings.

Parts of Cornwall, The Marches and East Anglia still used the dock to the end of the horse era.

A pair of London railway horses in pole harness. Double reins and skeleton harness, i.e. no breechings, are worn. Compare the amount of hair, or feather, on the legs with that of the modern Shire. (*Radio Times Hulton*)

Earlier forms of breechings also had a much deeper breech band, as much as 7 in deep in parts of the Welsh borders. In later years breechings became much lighter, the breech band seldom exceeding 3 to 4 in. It is doubtful if the earlier massive breechings were any stronger or more lasting, but their enormous weight could hardly have added to the comfort of the horse.

The pattern of breechings made in eastern Kent and the borders of Sussex and Surrey had a shorter breech band and were known as quoilers or coilers. This local word is said to have originated because of the way the breech band coils round something like the shape of a quoit, after they have been in use for some time. Another feature of the quoilers is the use of double hip straps, a feature not found anywhere else in the country.

Patterns are fairly standard over the rest of Britain. The Scottish pattern, perhaps, deserves separate mention. Here the single crupper strap is replaced by two thinner bearer straps sewn on to a large ring, which also takes the hip straps. The front end of the bearers are provided with small chains to loop over hooks attached to the back of the saddle bridge.

Breechings were also attached to the saddle on top of the housing in the north east and as far south as Lincolnshire. Over the rest of the country the practice was to attach them to a strap or leather loop fitted underneath the housing.

The long breechings of the pole harness for the Yorkshire wagons has a very long crupper which buckles to meeter straps over the hames. The chains from the breech band are also extra long so that they could be attached to the hame hooks as described earlier (see Chapter Four). They were seldom worn except when going into town. The system of backing these wagons appears to have been a precarious one for the wagoner. As the horses pushed back, the front of the pole tended to rise in the air. To stop this the wagoner stood on the pole and using the bearing reins balanced himself and urged the horses back. With a heavy load to back he was often standing above the horses' heads!

Except in Scotland, where the breechings were easily detachable, the saddle and breechings were removed from the horse as one and kept hanging together in the stable till needed again.

CHAPTER SIX

Yoking to Plough And Trace Harness

PLOUGH AND TRACE HARNESS

We have seen earlier that the plough harness, apart from the bridle and collar, simply consists of a back-band or plough band to hold up the trace chains. Though areas of Kent and East Anglia use a light hemp back-band, or beckit, generally they are of leather. To prevent soreness, they were often padded at the point where they sit on the back of the horse. The two ends have hooks to attach to the trace chains, below the exact line of their draught, so that there is no downward pressure on the back-band when the horse is in a hard pull. The hooks are usually backed by a broader piece of leather, called a safe, and this keeps the chains from rubbing the horses sides. When working an in-foal mare in plough harness, the safe was often padded to prevent undue hurting. This padding was lined with linen or basil (undressed sheepskin) and stuffed with flock.

A set of trace harness is more elaborate, and though often used for ploughing, especially at ploughing matches when it is used for attaching the decorations, it is more often seen worn by the trace horse giving extra power to the horse between the shafts. The set consists of a long crupper attached to the collar and kept in place by the use of a dock under the horse's tail. A separate back-band, similar to the plough-band, crosses the crupper in the middle of the back.

Hip straps are also provided, being attached to the crupper. Sometimes a second set of hip straps extended back behind the horse, to fasten to the trace chains at a spreader (a wooden bar fixed between the trace chains to hold them apart). The back-band and hip straps hold up the chains when not in a hard pull, and like the back-band of the plough harness, should not take any of the weight of the pull. As the draught of a horse in trace chains is more horizontal, a belly band is worn, and this prevents the horse's collar being pulled up against its windpipe.

Variations to the general pattern occur in the north east of England and parts of Scotland. Here the single long crupper is replaced by two straps at the top of the rump and passing either side of the shoulders to couple either to the draught hooks, or to the trace chains close to the hooks.

As a general rule, plough harness was used when coupling, or yoking horses abreast, and trace harness when yoking in line, one in front of the other.

YOKING IN PAIRS

The most common way of yoking horses to their draught was in pairs. For the trace horse, this meant being attached to the shafts of the cart or wagon, just in front of the shaft horse. Metal staples were provided at the ends of the shafts for this purpose. A trace horse was often needed to help another horse pull its load over soft ground or up steep hills.

On some busy city streets where a steep hill had to be negotiated, a permanent trace horse was kept at the bottom to help loads up the hill. In many cases its use was made compulsory and a small fee charged to cover costs. An article in *Saddlery and Harness* describes how the trace horse was replaced by a mechanical substitute in one part of London:

'Outside the Crystal Palace High Level Station stands a little traction engine called the "Little Giant", or better known as the "Horse's Friend". It is provided by the S.P.C.A. for any carman needing a pull up the very steep hills in the vicinity. It has assisted as many as forty vehicles of all sorts, from coal trolleys to pantechnicons, in one day.'

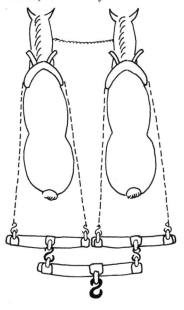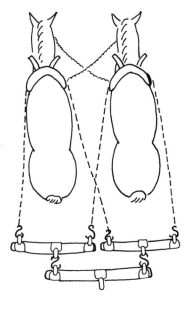

Fig 26 (*left*) Simple yoking of two horses abreast—each pulling on its own draught bar; (*right*) Yoking two horses so that each pulls on both draught bars

But the trace horse was not always so hard worked. In the north east of Scotland, for a horseman to be seen with only one horse, it was assumed that he was the orra boy working the orra, or spare, horse (see p. 110). So, no matter how light his load may be, if he was taking a cart on the road the horseman always took his 'pair' with him, the one dressed in trace harness. An article in a local paper 100 years ago, complained of the congestion caused in the town's streets by all the carts being pulled by two horses when only one was necessary.

In the south west of Scotland, trace harness and trace horses were almost unknown. Mr. Smith, of Biggar, never made a set of trace harness in his sixty years in the harness making trade.

Some horses were better than others as tracers, or leaders. For Watto Watson in the Lake District, 'a good trace horse needed to have more go in him—a bit of vice or unrulyness. This would keep him forward and the traces tight.' Geoff Morton, still farming with horses in Yorkshire, also explained how 'the leader needs to be keener than any of the others in any strung out yoking, in order to keep the traces tight. For that reason we often used a half-bred because they were usually livelier.'

Yoking two horses abreast necessitates the use of swingle-trees, or whipple-trees; 'a set of levers arranged as to cause the united strength of the horses to be exerted in one point'. Yoked to a set of swingle-trees, each horse has to pull just as much as its partner, which is particularly useful when going round corners. The first representation of a swingle-tree appears in the eleventh century on the Bayeux Tapestry. Mostly they were made of wood, oak being the most durable, but iron was rapidly replacing the wood when the horse era finished.

As an added precaution to prevent one horse pulling in front of the other, each horse is tied back from its inside bit ring to the inside hame of its partner. By this method of cross coupling neither horse can move in front of the other.

The simple form of attaching each horse to its own draught bar of the swingle-tree was the most widely used method of coupling two horses abreast (Fig. 26). All the ploughing with single furrow ploughs on medium and light land was done in this yoke. The left-hand horse walks on the untouched ground and is known as the land horse, whilst its partner walks in the channel left when the previous furrow was turned and is known as the furrow horse. The ploughman has a good view between the horses, and the plough can be set so that the beam also follows a straight line between them.

THREE-HORSE YOKING

The simple arrangement of a pair abreast becomes more complicated when a third horse is needed to pull a single furrow plough. As it is necessary to avoid the horses walking on the land already ploughed, the furrow horse must still walk in the bottom of the furrow. The third horse, therefore, has to be attached at the other side of the land horse. A third draught bar is fixed to the double swingle-tree by a further cross-bar which is attached to the plough one third of its length from the double swingle-trees (Fig. 27).

In this way all three horses are made to pull equally on the point of attachment to the plough. This point is now immediately behind the middle horse, though the line of the single furrow plough is still between the middle horse and the furrow horse. Therefore, when

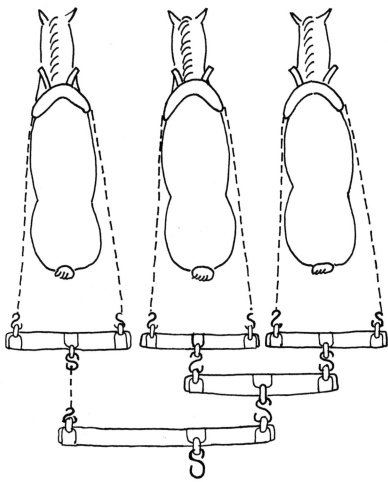

Fig 27
Three horse yoking
abreast

setting the plough it is necessary to allow for a pull to the left. This means that some of the power of the third horse is lost in counter-acting this sidewards pull.

The compensating set of swingle-trees for three horses is a much neater arrangement but was less popular because of its greater cost (Fig. 28). By moving the bolt at A to the left or right on the compensating lever, it is possible to lighten or make heavier the pull which the inside horse must exert. Similarly the load can be altered for either of the other horses. By moving both bolts at A and B outwards, the load on the central horse can be made lighter, which could be a useful arrangement when training a young horse to the team.

As with yoking horses to a two-horse swingle-tree, the traces

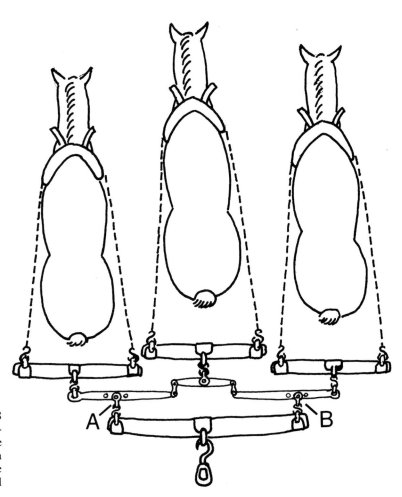

Fig 28
Compensating swingle-trees—by which the amount of work given to each horse could be varied

A three-horse set of swingle-trees in iron. These horses wear cruppers and hip straps which keep the chains from catching in the horses' feet when turning. (M.E.R.L)

can be crossed, so that each horse is pulling on two different draught bars. But this system is too complicated for practical use, and if the centre horse should slacken its pace, each of the outer pair has to take more of the load on its outside shoulder.

A simple method of attaching a third horse to a pair yoked to a two-horse swingle-tree, is by running a chain from the point of attachment to the plough, through between the horses, and attaching a single draught bar to the other end (Fig. 29). To this are attached the traces of the third horse. Known as unicorn fashion, the disadvantage of this method is that there is no way of equalising the pull of the third horse to the other two. It has the advantage, however, of all the power being used to pull the plough forward, there being no sidewards pull.

Pairs of horses harnessed to a vehicle with a central pole were often provided with extra power by attaching a third horse, unicorn fashion, to a draught bar fitted to the front of the pole. This was often done with the Yorkshire Pole Wagons.

Three horses can also be yoked to a wagon with a single pair of shafts by attaching draught bars at the end of each shaft and yoking a pair of horses separately in front of the shaft horse.

Yoking three horses bodkin fashion was a method used in parts of Yorkshire, Lincolnshire and Norfolk, for ploughing heavy land. Two horses walked in the furrow and one on the land (Fig. 30). The two-horse swingle-trees were provided with an iron crab, along which the crab hook could be moved to a position one third

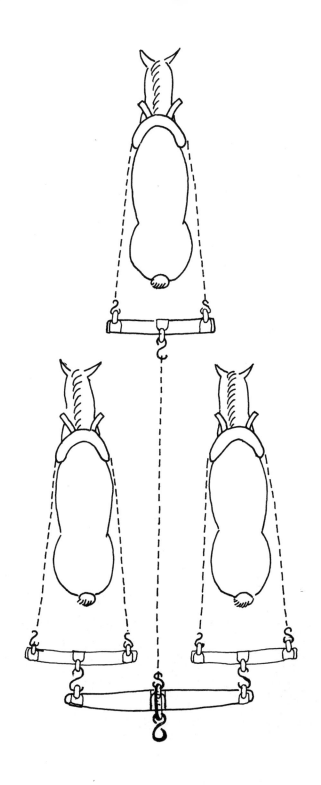

Fig 29
Unicorn Yoking of
three horses

of the length of the maisle tree (Fig. 31). This compensated for the two furrow horses pulling on a single draught bar.

Yoking three or more horses in line was practised when ploughing heavy clay lands, especially under wet conditions. It was also used extensively for attaching horses to large wagons, particularly timber wagons. Jimmy Chesshire, a retired Shropshire wagoner, generally ploughed with his horses yoked abreast, 'but come wet, we would always plough single (in line). The bottom of the furrow was firmer for the horses to walk on than the land to be ploughed. It also prevented the unploughed land being puddled.'

The *General Dictionary of Husbandry*, 1766 gave the following list of disadvantages of ploughing in line. First, the setting of the plough was not natural, the pull being to the right of the line of the furrow. It was thus necessary to give the plough more land, making it heavier to pull and more difficult to control. Secondly, some horses are lazier than others and it is easier for them to get away with not pulling their share of the weight than if yoked abreast. Thirdly, the hindmost horse has to bear a downward weight on its back because of the change in angle of the draught chains from the front horses.

Ideally, to provide each horse with its best angle of draught, each would need a separate set of traces to the plough. As this would be too cumbersome—turning the team would be an impossibility—all the horses have to pull on traces coupled together to form a single line of draught. For the front two horses the traces are horizontal, but the horse nearest the plough has to take the downward thrust

Horses yoked to a binder unicorn fashion, *c*.1900. The far horse of the pair is in shafts and wears full shaft harness. Note the Kentish Style of breechings. The boy riding postillion was once a common practice. (*Radio Times Hulton*)

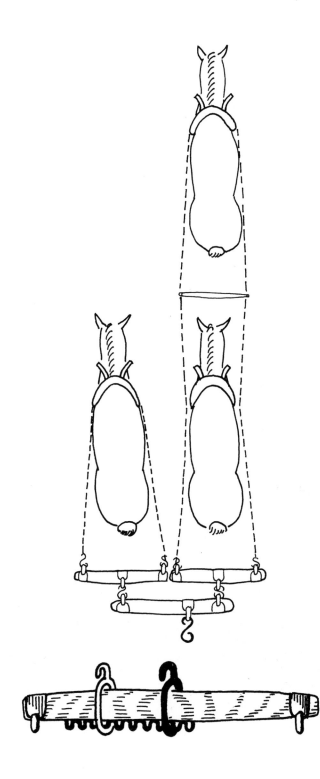

Fig 30
Yoking horses bodkin
fashion

Fig 31
Maisle tree for two
horse swingle-trees—
with adjustable crab
hook for working bodkin
fashion

caused by the change in the angle of draught between it and the plough (Fig. 32). In areas where yoking in line was most practised, special devices were used to overcome this. The hind horse wore its cart saddle, and in the heavy Wealden clays of Kent, the redger iron took the weight of the trace chains on to the saddle and at the same time kept the chains away from the horse's sides. Similarly in Herefordshire and Shropshire the saddled hind horse had its bends and traces.

The front horses were usually harnessed in trace harness and the traces kept apart by spreaders, though many wagoners just yoked their horses in line in ordinary plough harness quite successfully.

The methods employed for coupling each horse's traces to those of the horse behind varied. Some were coupled as near to the draught hooks of the following horse as possible. Others were coupled to a spare link provided in the traces as much as 2 ft 6 in behind draught hooks.

Fig 32
Working in line—with horse nearest plough wearing its cart saddle with a 'redger' iron to take the weight of the downward thrust caused by the change in the line of draught

Many farmers used in-line ploughing when training a young horse. With a good strong horse in front and behind, a young horse had little alternative but to keep its place in the middle. In any event, an extra strong horse was needed in the hind position because, when the end of the furrow was reached, it had to pull the plough

out on its own, the front horses having turned down the line of the headland.

FOUR-HORSE YOKING

If extra heavy conditions demanded the use of a fourth horse, for in line working, this would just mean attaching it in front of the three-horse team, but the problems associated with in line working were increased.

Four horses yoked abreast were frequently used for pulling heavy harrows. Two double swingle-trees were coupled either end of a master-tree to give the necessary set up for each horse to pull equally. But it was impossible for four horses to plough abreast without the furrows being trampled, so two pairs of horses coupled one behind the other, were frequently used. Again, it was in the Weald and other areas of heavy clays that four horses yoked in two pairs, were most likely to be seen.

The most popular method was similar to that described for the unicorn yoking except that the chain running between the back pair, called a soam, had to be stronger, and a double set of swingle-trees were fitted to the front for the foremost pair of horses. The soam chain was kept in position by two short chains from the collars

Four horses ploughing a single furrow in line, Kent 1926. It was more usual to find the horse nearest the plough wearing a cart saddle, with a redger iron to take the weight of the downward pull of the traces. (M.E.R.L)

of the hind pair of horses. Because each pair was yoked separately to the plough, either pair could make their work easier by making the other pull the harder. To overcome this, ways were devised whereby each pair of horses was coupled to the other pair by a pulley, and so each individual horse had to take its share of the draught. This system was made more complicated by the need for a check chain to stop either pair getting too far behind.

By far the simplest method of yoking four horses in two pairs seems only to have been introduced to this country in recent years. It had been used in America and Canada during the horse era but for some reason was never taken up in this country until Geoff Morton, recently imported an American two furrow riding plough to his farm in Yorkshire together with instructions on yoking four-horse teams. The method used is simply a four-horse swingle-tree worked out on the same principles as the three-horse one (Fig. 33). The front pair of horses share a simple two-horse swingle-tree, and by means of a long chain these in turn share a three-horse swingle-tree with the hind furrow horse, and together they share a four-horse swingle-tree with the hind land horse. In this way all four horses share the draught equally, without any complicated system of pulleys.

Four horses yoked in pairs to a two-way, double-furrow plough with rope traces and light, hemp back hands. The heavy soam chain from the leading swingle-tree to the plough is visible. Note how the rear pair of horses hold up the swingle-tree of the leading pair—Thanet ploughing match, 1950. (M.E.R.L)

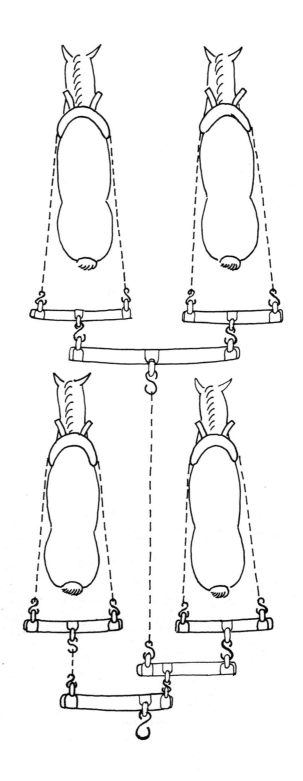

Fig 33
Yoking four horses
American fashion

Multiple yokes, or hitches, of more than four horses were not often used in this country. It would be too complicated to devise a system where each horse pulled an equal share of the draught so multiples of one or other of the yokings already described were used.

The only team of eight horses in this country; the team of black Shires from Young's brewery, Wandsworth in London. The leading three pairs are all yoked to the same traces.
(*Young & Co.*)

An American hitch of eight Clydesdales. Each pair has its own set of swingle-trees attached to a pole which is held up by the following pair of horses. Note the peaked collars, not unlike those worn by the Clydesdales in their home country.
(*Anheuser Busch Inc.*)

CHAPTER SEVEN

The Harness Makers

GENERAL CONDITIONS OF THE TRADE

The multiplicity of patterns of heavy horse harness which were made throughout the country, started life in the shops of the town and country saddler and harness-maker. Most cart-horse harness was made in small establishments, smelling of wax and leather, seldom employing more than two or three assistants and very often only the proprietor himself. The country saddler and harness-maker was a respected and essential member of the community and, like so many of his brother craftsmen, scratched a precarious living by the skill of his hands. It was not a prosperous trade, the farmers particularly being notorious for wanting the best job at the cheapest price and taking up to twelve months to pay for the work. Though many country harness-makers showed great skill in the making of the more fancy and more profitable carriage harness, on the whole these people who could afford to have their own carriages went to the more fashionable city saddlers for new trappings. The poor country saddler was left to make a living as best he could from repair work and the making of the heavier cart harness.

Again, like so many of their brother craftsmen, the harness-makers were too weak to combine to fix prices which would give them a reasonable return for their labours. Instead, undercutting was rife amongst them. A saddler sadly writes in 1891, 'There is not one trade in existance that is so poor and never makes headway. I start work at 6 a.m. and work until 9.30 p.m. every day in the week to try and get on. Saddlers need to unite to keep up their prices and get a reasonable return.' Most saddlers were too proud to reduce the quality of their work in order to fight the under-cutting of prices and the result was an unusually high incidence of bankruptcy in the trade. This was particularly so at the end of the last century, even when the use of the heavy horse was at its height, and once the decline in horse numbers set in so the bankruptcy rate increased.

It would seem that the experienced craftsmen often lacked a business sense and failed to realise when they were charging too little for their work. Costings formed no part in their training as apprentices. Competitors who charged 6d. more for an article were regarded as extortionists, and those who charged 6d. less were looked upon as doing an inferior class of trade. Even after the formation of regional Saddlers Associations at the turn of the century, there was little improvement in the situation. And a great deal of the problem lay in the multiplicity of different local patterns of heavy horse harness.

With the decline in the harness trade, many saddlers looked elsewhere for work to keep their shops busy. One such job was the making and repairing of binder canvasses. The binder arrived from America at the turn of the century, and the canvasses conveyed the cut corn through the binder before the tied sheaves were thrown out at the side. The canvasses were in constant need of repair and Mr. Smith of Biggar has records of 14 000 canvasses made or repaired passing through his shop since 1926.

George Bell of Cupar in Fife turned his hand to shoe repairing when the harness trade disappeared, achieving a high standard of skill and reaching championship standard when entering his work

The country saddler could turn his skill to making most types of harness and saddlery, but his chief source of income seems to have come from the repair of harness. Too often he was required to bring back to life old and worn harness fit only for the fire.
(C. F. Snow)

in competitions. The recent revival of horse riding and the demand for saddlery enabled him, and so many like him, to return to the trade they were first taught. Because of the uncertainty of the trade after the last war, few young apprentices came into it, with the result that today the average age of the country saddler must be approaching retiring age. Those people who have kept the heavy horse and those who are wanting to bring them back on a small scale are experiencing great difficulty in finding the men who are capable of repairing, let alone making, the heavy horse harness.

Though most of the large farms, and many small ones too, looked after their harness, the country harness-maker seems to have been bedevilled with having to repair harness which had been badly treated. Letters from country saddlers at the turn of the century complain bitterly of the condition of some of the harness. One writes: 'The old rubbish that is brought to be repaired is often completely worn out and ought to have been destroyed years ago. But you must do the best you can, and there is so much to be done in a given time, you have to bodge it and draw it together in anything but a workman-like manner.'

Another correspondent writes: 'The majority of British farmers evidently think that leather ought to wear for ever, since they lump down a lot of last-century tackle in various saddler's shops to be repaired. Marvellously the country saddler somehow puts life into these seemingly hopeless rubbish heaps and starts the farmer's harnish on another century's wear.'

The advent of binder twine and baling wire was a boon to these make-shift farmers. Many temporary repairs were performed on the harness using string or wire—often to the great discomfort of the horses. Describing such a farmer, Mr. Brown of Elwick in Durham said, 'he yokes up with Charlie Turner and looses out with a knife'. Charlie Turner was the name of a local string firm.

Too many farmers seemed not to realise the importance of keeping harness in good condition. Many used harness for years without once giving it a dressing of oil, and many never bothered to clean off the mud and sweat. The neglected leather would become brittle and too often the harness-maker was blamed. Harness should be thoroughly cleaned and oiled, at the very least, once a year, and mud, manure and sweat should not be allowed to work into the pores of the leather.

THE HARNESS-MAKER'S MATERIALS

The harness-maker uses many different types of leather, each having its own purpose. For Noel Davies of Much Wenlock, the leather used for making heavy harness was known as gear back and that for lighter harness as harness back; both being made from cowhide. His leather came already dressed and dyed, 'though we had to finish off the edges ourselves'. In the dressing of the leather the manufacturers worked in a lot of grease—'Cod Island tallow'.

Many saddlers preferred to dress their own skins, and indeed at one time many went as far as to do their own slaughtering and skinning. The word knacker, as applied to the slaughtering trade, had its origins in the saddlery and harness craft. Ewart Evans describes the word knacker as coming from an Islandic root, Knakkr, meaning a saddle.

A saddler writes, in 1903; in *Saddlery and Harness*: 'I was apprenticed to the trade in 1839. At that time many country saddlers spun their own ropes, dressed their white leather, killed and skinned horses and were frequently called knackers.' This use of the word knacker as applied to a saddler seems to have been limited to the eastern half of the country.

Country Saddler and Currier's Shop at Falmouth, *c*.1910. The country saddler sold all sorts of leather goods and stable fittings from his shop besides harness. (M.E.R.L)

Another name sometimes used for the saddler was a wittaw; i.e. one who dresses white leather. White leather is usually horsehide and dressed with alum. It is never tanned. At one time most of the harness was made from well dressed white leather, but later its use was limited to thongs for stitching the body of the collar to the outside covering, and was known as whit-(white)thong.

Most leather used in later years has been tanned cow-hide, and even this seems to have changed in quality over the years. Many harness-makers have complained of the reduced quality of the leather caused by animals being killed younger for beef and not being kept for their hides. Also, the speeding up of the tanning process meant a poorer quality leather. The best leather is said to be that which has been through a pure oak tan.

If the leather is bought in whole hides, the best parts of the hide— across the back and sides of the animal—are used for new harness, whilst the belly part is used for repairs, linings and fillings. As the hides are much stronger lengthways, straps are never cut across the hide. In cutting a hide for cart harness, the best is used for the breeching straps then the crupper, followed by the hip straps, and then the cart belly bands and bridle. The best part of the belly can be used for the side-pieces of the collar. Special curried leather is used for the cart saddle housings and for blinkers as the ordinary harness leather contains too much oil and is not firm enough.

For cart harness the leather is dyed black and the colour will not be spoilt by the constant greasing necessary to keep the harness supple. One recipe for the dye is given by Hasluck: 'boil together logwood chips, crushed nutgalls, copperas, a little gum arabic and water'.

Patent harness work for the heavy horse is seen only in the cities and japanned hides are needed for this.

American cloth is a glazed, coated cloth once used by many harness-makers for facing the harness, in the swelled cheeks of stallion bridles and for the backing of face-pieces and martingales to show up the brasses.

Flock is a mixture of materials such as wool fibres, horse-hair and goat hair, and is used for stuffing collars. A flocking machine is used to loosen the fibres. Alternatively drummed flock can be used from the roll, and being of even thickness is best for lining a. collar before stuffing with straw. Rye straw is the best for stuffing collars, and though a lot was once grown in this country, most has long been imported from the Continent. Felt is used to line the underside of cruppers or under any straps likely to chafe the horses skin. In some counties the insides of the cheek-straps are so lined.

Most saddlers make their own waxed threads using hemp and home-made wax. The word hemp was not used everywhere; many harness-makers preferring to call it lint, maintaining that hemp was a coarse substitute imported from Russia and Manila, and used mostly for ropemaking. The threads are made up according to the strength required, varying from three to sixteen strands of hemp. The saddler twists the hemp into a thread by rubbing it across the top of his knee with the palm of his hand. Any lumps in the resulting thread are smoothed out by drawing the blade of an awl backwards and forwards across the thread. For coarse work and repairs it is unnecessary to smooth out the thread but it must be waxed with cobblers wax made by melting resin and pitch and mixing with a little linseed-oil. The thread is first rubbed with the wax and then with a soft leather to spread the wax evenly. The inseparable combination of the saddler and his ball of wax originated the term waxy, meaning a saddler, in the army. Waxing the thread protects it and gives it a longer life. It also helps to hold the stitching tightly in the leather. After waxing, the thread is ready for use.

The use of whit-thong for stitching collars has already been mentioned, but at one time thonging was extensively used for sewing the harness together—though not altogether successfully, according to Lisle in his *Husbandry*, 1713: 'Everybody grows weary of harness worked up with thongs for, though it looks pretty at first, it soon flies to pieces.'

THE HARNESS-MAKER'S TOOLS

Most of the saddler's tools are individual to their trade, but at the same time show little variation within the different workshops over the country (Fig. 34).

The following tools are standard throughout the trade though the names used probably show some variation.

The round knife: this ancient half-moon knife is probably the most distinctive of the saddler's tools. Great skill is required in its use and many saddlers would use no other knife. It is one of the most useful tools to the harness-maker for cutting out, paring down ends for splicing and a variety of other work. The double headed knife is smaller than the round knife. It is always made with one point more extended and acute than the other—to suit the different types of work. It is used for cutting out blinkers and for rounded or scalloped work. The paring knife is a useful all-round knife for cutting threads, paring down and splicing. The collar knife is slightly larger and is used for trimming off surplus straw.

Edge trimmers are used to round off the sharp edges of the leather and are used in various sizes. The saddler's spokeshave is suitable for thinning light straps and for trimming work such as back bands. Slitting machines split strips of leather into a uniform thickness. The plough gauge completes the list of cutting tools and is used for cutting leather into parallel strips—doing the job more evenly than is possible by hand.

Fig 34
The Harness-maker's tools

The tools for setting out work and marking it include the older

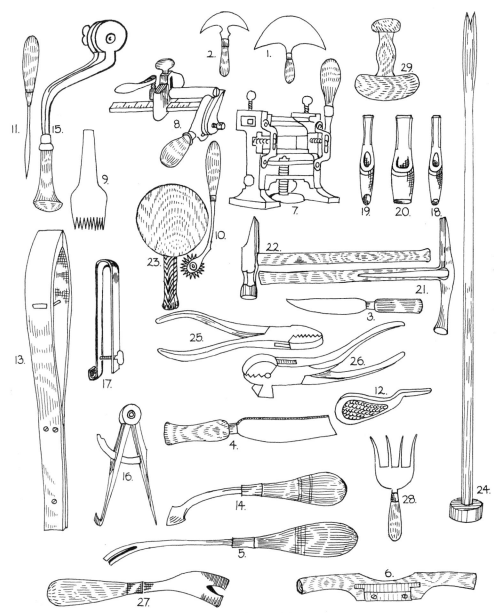

1. Round knife
2. double headed knife
3. paring knife
4. collar knife
5. edge trimmer
6. spokeshave
7. slitting machine
8. plough gauge

9. pricking iron
10. pricking wheel
11. awl
12. palm iron
13. Saddler's vice
14. single crease
15. Shoulder vein
16. Compass racer

17. Screw racer
18. round punch.
19. oval punch
20. crew punch
21. Saddler's hammer
22. riveting hammer
23. collar maker's mallet
24. collar stuffing iron

25. Bulcher's pliers
26. Saddler's pincers
27. nail claw
28. cross web
    straining fork
29. Smasher.

straight pricking iron and the more recent pricking wheel. Though the pricking wheel is much quicker to use, many saddlers kept to the straight pricking iron because they believed them to be superior. By hitting the pricking iron quite firmly the holes are made deeper and the stitching can be done more easily, and in this way lost time is recovered. Pricking irons and wheels are designed to mark the leather from 6 to 16 per inch, and in the holes made by the teeth the harness is stitched. Many skilled harness-makers ignore the use of pricking irons and work by eye and skill alone. The saddler also requires an assortment of stitching awls for boring the holes for the needles.

Various types and thicknesses of needle are used for stitching with waxed thread and all other stitching threads. Special collar needles up to 6 in long are needed for heavy cart collar work. These heavier needles require a palm iron to drive them through the thick collar leather. The palm iron is equivalent to a thimble, except that it is held in the palm of the hand.

To hold work for stitching, a pair of clambs, or saddler's vice is used. This simple clamp is held between the saddler's knees. It is usually constructed of oak (often two oak barrel staves were used) and the two bowed jaws meet tightly at the top. The saddler has to pull the jaws apart to insert his work and keeps the pressure up by squeezing the vice between his knees as he sews.

Sewing machines: the first machine for sewing leather with a waxed thread was produced by Pearsons of Leeds in 1867. At first the machine was ridiculed by the harness trade, though the shoe trade were not slow to bring it into use. The harness trade abroad bought it in large numbers, but over twenty years were to pass before it became accepted in this country. Even then only the large manufacturers used them. Most of the country harness-makers were too small to invest in machinery and, even after the turn of the century, they were still arguing as to whether they were a good thing or not. Those who did venture to use the sewing machines had nothing but praise for them:

'After twelve years of using sewing machines, I have yet to see the first piece of work which has been a discredit to me for either wear or appearance. A good sewing machine is a slave who never complains and will do more work before breakfast than a stitcher can do all day' (*Saddlery and Harness*, 1911).

The use of rivets came from America about 1890, where harness was often made using rivets almost exclusively. The British harness-makers, however, scorned their use for all but a few specialised jobs.

To mark the lines for the stitching, screw creases, adjustable to bring the line nearer or father away from the edge of the work, are used. The single crease is used mainly for ornamental work, though the single or double lines ornamenting the straps, and so favoured by the saddlers north of the border, are made by heated creasing irons. The heavier shoulder vein gives a better purchase for this kind of creasing work.

The compass and screw racers are tools for cutting out a shallow groove in the leather so that the stitching is sunk below the surface.

Various sizes and shapes of punches are needed for the work of the harness-maker. Round punches are used for holes in bridle straps and other light strap work; oval punches are needed for heavier harness work—the oval shape gives the size of hole required without weakening the leather to the extent that a similarly sized round punch would. The crew punch cuts an oblong, rounded at the end, and is used for making the holes in which the heel of the buckle tongue needs to move freely.

Other tools found on the harness-maker's work-bench include a saddler's hammer and a riveting hammer. A heavy wooden collar mallet, made from lignum-vitae, and occasionally iron, takes a lot of muscle-power for it can weigh up to 7 lb. It is used for pummelling the collar stuffing carefully into the required shape as the work proceeds. Although it appears to be perfectly round when seen from the front, in fact one of the faces of the mallet is flatter than the others.

The collar-makers also need special tools for packing the straw filling into the forewhale and the body of the collar. They are known as stuffing irons and come in different lengths up to 2 ft 6 in. The jimmy is a similar tool for the lighter collar work.

Bulcher's pliers with sharks jaws are most useful for taking a firm grip of the leather when stretching it. There are other patterns of pliers and pinchers which the saddler finds useful. Nail claws are handy for removing nails, and the cross web straining fork speaks for itself.

One of the most unusual tools used by the saddler is a smasher. It is used for rubbing down stitching and setting blinker linings firmly to the metal stiffening plate. Like the collar-maker's mallet, it too is made from lignum-vitae.

The blocking of the blinkers to form the raised patterns is done by a blinker, or winker press which moulds the wetted leather between a pair of gunmetal blocks. Various patterns from scallop shells to deep round bosses are to be found, though each area tended to keep to a local traditional style. The purpose of blocking the blinker, apart from decoration, is to give more room for air to circulate around the horse's eyes.

The above tool kit is completed with a good box-wood ruler, and such unlikely items as 'one or two bones for rubbing up the edges of the leather'.

THE WORK OF THE HARNESS-MAKER

To describe in full the makings of a set of heavy horse harness would take a book in itself, and the reader is referred to accounts already written on the subject. However, there are many aspects of the harness-maker's work which are worth recording as they will not be found in a purely technical account of the making of a set of harness.

Usually the first skills an apprentice was taught was how to make and wax the hemp threads and then how to stitch. The whole of this first year would be spent stitching until he could do the work neatly. Later he was taught the best and most economic way to cut out the harness from the hides, with the thickest parts used for those pieces of the harness taking the most wear.

Most apprentices served seven years with very little pay. Mr. Cooper, saddler, of Bridlington, recalls his father saying that for the six years after being apprenticed he worked for nothing but his keep and the privilege of being taught the trade. During this time his mother was sent 6d. each week.

Towards the end of their term of apprenticeship, many lads took part in feats of skill by producing miniature pieces of harness, exact in every detail. Many were used as window pieces in the saddlers' shops before finally finding their way into museums. In parts of Scotland, model horses were harnessed in miniature before the apprentice passed out to become a journeyman or day-worker. Competitions were also held to determine who could make the most stitches to the inch. This called for very fine work, especially if the stitching were to be done without weakening the leather.

The journeyman was usually expected to provide his own set of tools—apart from the more expensive ones such as plough gauges and slitting machines.

The harness trade tended to be a family trade and father was followed by son whenever possible, and as the trade declined between the wars many sons did not complete the full seven years apprenticeship. The result was that when the revival in the saddlery trade came, due solely to the increasing popularity of riding, there were not enough trained saddlers left to fulfill the orders. Recent efforts by the trade to correct the position have not been completely successful and the demand for skilled saddlers is still acute.

Each saddler could identify his own workmanship even years

after the piece of harness had passed through his skilled hands. Not only could they tell from the pattern used, but also by the actual stitching. Many too learnt to recognise their competitors' work, which wasn't always too difficult as most harness-makers went out of their way to place a trade mark of some sort on their craftsmanship. On bridles in England and Wales this was usually done by advertising their name and address on a brass nose-band plate. In Scotland the harness-makers preferred to use smaller shield designs chosen from hundreds of patterns provided by the manufacturers' catalogues.

Other saddlers preferred to mark their leather work with a punch imprinting the information of their whereabouts. Saddlers around the counties of Shropshire, Cheshire and Lancashire were fond of using this method of identification. Less informative trade marks by way of simple patterns cut in steel punches were used to decorate the harness by saddlers as far apart as Penzance, east Yorkshire and Shrewsbury, up to recent times.

Some saddlers preferred to put their fancy work into the stitching —especially where double thicknesses of leather needed to be reinforced.

Not all the work was done on the premises. Most country saddlers would travel out to the bigger farms at regular intervals to overhaul the harness—usually during a lull in the farming calendar. This often meant leaving about 6 a.m. to be ready to start at the farm by 7 a.m. They would have to carry all the tools and materials they would be likely to use. To have to return to the shop for forgotten tools or materials would mean valuable time and money lost. The harness-maker would charge the farmer by the day. For Mr. Cooper's father this was £1 per day for his own labour, that of a lad, and also all materials used. He would set up a bench in one of the barns and on a big farm there could be enough work, by way of repairs, to keep him going for a week.

Noel Davies recalls that, when visiting the farms, as they repaired the harness, so the men on the farm were 'ordered to oil the leather and buckles with cod oil—especially any parts where rusting could occur. Rusting would crack the leather and cause it to break as if it had been burnt'.

The country saddler had to be able to turn his hand to any kind of leather work. For Noel Davies the work in his younger days was fairly evenly divided between heavy horse harness, the lighter trap harness, and brown saddlery—i.e. the making of riding bridles and saddles.

Not only did the type of work vary, but some harness-makers living on the watershed of two or more regional patterns, would have to be in a position to be able to produce either pattern, if required. Gordon Lancaster, of Penrith, could make harness of the local Scottish style as well as those of the nearby Lancashire and Yorkshire styles.

The quality of work of some harness-makers became known far beyond the usual boundaries of a country saddler. Prentice of Carluke was one who became known over the whole of Scotland—especially for his decorated plough bands, used by many competitors to adorn their pair of horses at ploughing matches. George Bell of Cupar—before he was forced to turn to shoe repairs—became noted for his high quality of show harness for the heavy Clydesdales. In 1945 he began making show harness as an advertisement and came to enjoy the work so much that he regarded it as a labour of love. As he found the ordinary cart harness leather too greasy for the show harness, he used leather that had been tanned but not dressed. 'The main thing was to get it black; it didn't matter what you polished it with afterwards.' By 1946 he had achieved remarkable success for a paragraph in the Scottish Farmer of July that year reads: 'Mr. Geo. Bell, saddler of Bonnygate, Cupar, achieved a notable success at Cupar Angus show. The first 3 prize-winning sets of harness—the best in the field—were made by him. The judges spoke highly of his work.'

The Scottish harness-makers, in general, were renowned for their quality of work. In the harness making competitions organised by the trade journal Saddlery and Harness, the Scots almost monopolised the gold and silver medals awarded. Their fame spread abroad too, and the Scottish pattern of heavy horse harness spread to parts of America and to those countries in the Commonwealth where the heavy horse was introduced. Many Scots emigrated to these developing countries and brought their skilled craft with them.

As the trade began to decline and fewer young men learnt the craft, many saddlers looked to the traveller from Walsall, who at one time always dressed in a top hat and frock-coat, to supply them with some of the heavier work connected with the making of the cart harness. When making a set of harness for a customer they would send to Walsall for the collar body and even the complete cart saddle, leaving only the collar covering and strap work to do themselves.

Walsall had grown up as the centre of manufacture of complete sets as well as all the harness fittings and decorations, and the tools which the harness-makers needed to carry on their craft.

CHAPTER EIGHT

Wagoners and Other Horsemen

MEN DEVOTED TO HORSES

No account of the heavy horse would be complete without mention of the men who devoted their lives to looking after the interests of those horses. The devotion of these men was so great that they have been known to give in their notice after many years of employment because a pair of horses in their charge had been sold off the premises.

As Bert Boulton of Herefordshire reflected, 'The horses was the only company you had all day. I had some happy times with horses, often working from five in the morning to ten at night with only the two horses for company. And they was company too. You knew all their little ways, and they knew yours.'

On farms where teams of horses were worked regularly, it was usual to find at least one man who was in charge of the horses and who worked with them and nothing else. He may have had assistants, but he himself was known as the wagoner, carter, horseman, horse-keeper, teamsman, or ploughman, depending on the part of the country in which he worked.

On the big arable farms where up to ten teams of horses might be worked, there was a hierarchy amongst the horsemen, with very strict patterns of behaviour. For example, the foreman horseman would invariably be the first to lead his team of horses out of the stable in the morning, and woe betide the underling who dared to lead his team outside in any but his correct station. The same order would be kept walking the horses to the field and in the field itself, if a number of teams were ploughing. Mr. Marshal Manson, of Brechin, Angus recalled this tradition. 'The stable was the focal point of the farms around here. In the mornings orders were given out in the stable and it was a sight to see the horses coming out of the stable at yoking time headed by the foreman, second man, third man etc. Putting on the harness was a really slick operation and traditionally the foreman was the slickest, followed by the second man, etc. and so they always left the stable in that order and returned from the field in a similar fashion.'

Even on relatively small farms in some areas the wagoner was responsible only for the horses and would never be expected to lift up a pitchfork at harvest time. Andrew Dunlop, of Pett in Sussex, remembers how 'the under-ploughman or under-carter was expected to do general work about the farm whilst the carter did nothing but see to the horses. He was too grand for doing other work and would walk around with the horses all day in the harvest field. When working the teams in a wagon on the roads, he had a boy to lead the trace horse whilst he himself lorded it over the lot, walking well back to be ready to put the squat (slipper or skidpan) under the wheel if needed.'

On the farms it was the wagoners or horsemen who looked after their horses, bedding them down, feeding and grooming them, both morning and evening, but this was an unusual arrangement to find in the towns. Here the drivers of the heavy delivery drays and council tip-carts were drivers only and the stables were run separately by others. In the Midlands the town drivers were known as carters, but their county cousins on the farms were wagoners.

On the large farms where a number of teams of horses were worked, there was usually a single horse kept either as a spare if a replacement were needed in one of the teams, or to do the odd jobs about the farm. This horse would be in charge of the apprentice lad, known in Northumberland as the turnip dick, because his chief job was to take the turnips out to the animals. Further north he would be known as the orra boy or, in Angus, the orra loon, the odd job horseman who worked the orra horse. He was not to be confused with that highly skilled worker on the farm who could turn his hand to anything and was known as the orra man.

At one time the wagoners went to the hiring fairs, or mops, to be hired and traditionally they wore a piece of whip lash in their caps to identify themselves as wagoners. Horsemen were probably the last of the farm 'trades' to be hired in this fashion, and long after the rest of the farm's employees had been enjoying a weekly wage, the horsemen found themselves still being hired for the year. In parts of Yorkshire the practice did not die out until as late as the 1950s.

Where the wagoners or horsemen, lived together in close communities, they gathered round them a mass of knowledge on the management of horses, some mystic but mostly sound practical information which they passed amongst each other. In some areas, especially in the north east of Scotland where the bothy system was prevalent, secret horseman's societies grew up to exchange such knowledge.

HORSEMEN AND SECRET SOCIETIES

In the bothy system the single men on the farm lived together in the bothy and there they slept, cooked and ate their meals, and there they made their own entertainment. These were usually the horsemen on large arable farms and in the confines of the bothy the Horsemen's Society grew up in the nineteenth century. The Society had much ritual and many secrets and was limited in membership to the horsemen themselves and occasionally the local blacksmith, as his premises were often used as a meeting place.

Only trusted horsemen were invited to be initiated as members and to persuade young lads to join, the old hands used various tricks, such as concealing a holly prickle in the collar lining of the young lad's horse. This would naturally make the horse very jumpy and the lad would be told that once he had the horseman's word everything would be all right. They were trained up for the initiation ceremony, usually performed at the dead of night in a location where they were unlikely to be disturbed. Entry fee, according to one Fife horseman was 'a bottle of whisky and a piece of Dundee cake'.

Much ritual took part at the ceremony, secret passwords were given and oaths taken not to reveal the horseman's word. A good party followed the proceedings and new recruits had information about horses freely given to them by their elders.

In Fife, if a member was 'having trouble with a difficult horse, he would call the Society together and, at night and without the farmer's knowledge, the horse was brought into a field on a long rope where they 'raried' it to cure it of its badness. After running it round till it tired, the horse was couped (thrown) and tormented by its handler until its temper was broken. The art was to make sure the horse knew he had been mastered but at the same time not to go too far and break its spirit'. Most farmers were against this practice and would sack any horseman discovered taking part.

Not all horsemen cared to join the Society, but most of the young bloods regarded membership as part of the process of being recognised as a man, and not just a lad, by their fellow horsemen. Many of the secrets passed amongst the members were involved with keeping the horses in the best possible condition, for though they were occasionally involved in some cruel practices, most of them were horsemen of the highest standards, who loved their horses and were experts in the art of handling them. Indeed, many believe that the finest horsemen in the world working with heavy horses came from this part of Scotland.

Many horsemen from north east Scotland sought positions, and eventually settled in East Anglia. Here the traces of similar Horsemen's Societies have been noted, but the East Anglian horsemen looked more to employing charms, such as a bone from a dead frog or toad, to give them the power they needed over their horses.

Horsemen all over Britain collected recipes with which they believed they were able to control not only the horse's health but also its physical movement. Recipes were known not only for stopping a horse in its tracks but also for attracting the horse to its handler. Oils from all imaginable sources were mixed together to create cures for all sorts of horse's ills.

Not all horsemen were 'made' with the elaborate ceremonies of the secret societies. Much more down to earth methods were employed in some counties, like Shropshire, where Jimmy Cheshire described his initiation as a wagoner: 'One day, when I was a lad, the old wagoner on the farm says to me, "If you want to be a wagoner young lad, you'll have to be christened, same as all us others was." With that someone lifted the tail of one of the old mares and I had my face well and truely rubbed into her backside. That's how I was made a wagoner. There was no secret society about it!'

WORKING WITH HORSES IN THE FIELD

Most horsemen started their careers very early in life, many of them working in the fields after school hours and during the school holidays. Their first job was usually that of leading the horses, especially where they were harnessed in line. One eighty-two-year-old Worcestershire wagoner remembers his first job as a boy was leading the front horse, and because he was so small, he was provided with a stick which had a piece of string attaching it to the lead horse's bit. Another old carter remembers his first job, as a ten year old, was to ride on the lead horse of a team coupled to a binder.

Later, when they left school and sought a permanent post on a farm, the young lads would be very keen to learn from the other horsemen, with ambitions to have their own pair of horses. So keen was Mr. Beard, when a lad in Oxfordshire, to try his hand at ploughing that, when one Sunday he was left to look after the farm, he seized the opportunity and harnessed two of the horses to a plough and tried to cut a furrow as he had watched the others do. He had been so sure that he could plough as well as the rest; but everything seemed to go wrong, and so disappointed was he with his first efforts, that he quickly returned the horses to the stable. Taking a spade he went back to the field and proceeded to turn the furrow back again by hand. The only comment next day from the wagoner was about the activity of the moles in the field!

But the lads progressed, and before he left that farm, Mr. Beard was able to set a plough, and if the field was right for the occasion, could send the horses on their own down the furrow to be met at the other end by one of the other men, who could set them off back up the field. They often tried this with two pairs of horses. Each would stand in the opposite headland and turn the horses, which had to be good steady ones, back down the next furrow. 'The ground needed to be fairly level and free of stones. A field which had had sheep folded on it was best. Once a plough was properly set it needed little handling. We could save ourselves a lot of miles that way.'

Jimmy Cheshire, and other good ploughmen, would often leave the plough and walk alongside their horses, but in the north of England and in Scotland, where the swing plough was used, this was not so easy as there was no wheel in the furrow to keep the plough from wandering.

As Ron Creasy, from Yorkshire, related, it was the foreman, or head horseman, who had the responsibility of setting out the rigs — measuring up the field and ploughing the first furrow. If the ridges had been set out properly and the first furrow straight, then the rest of the field would have straight parallel furrows from one end to the other. The headlands at either end of the field were usually five to six yards deep and these would be ploughed out at the finish 'right up to the roots of the hedge'.

Times of working in the field differed from county to county. Basically the country was divided into those areas which worked a single work period from 7 a.m. to 2.30 p.m., with a short break mid-morning, and those which worked a double shift, 7 a.m. to 12 p.m. and 1.30 p.m. to 5 p.m. The former system, known as a journey in Suffolk, single hooking in the West Midlands, or as working one yoke over most of the greater part of the country, is probably a survival of the days when oxen were used for ploughing. It was enough to yoke up oxen only once a day and to let them loose in the afternoon to recuperate for the following day's ploughing.

A typical day's timetable for a one yoke system would be: 5 a.m. feed and water horses and muck out stable; 6.30 a.m. horsemans breakfast; 7 a.m. to the fields, a half hour's break around 11 a.m.; 3 p.m. return horses to stable, unharness, and horseman goes for his dinner; back to the stable at 3.45 p.m. to feed, water and straw up the horse's beds. The horseman returned to the stable at 7 p.m. to water and feed the horses and shake up the bedding.

Over most of the country horses were kept in the stables over-night during the winter months, but in some eastern counties from Yorkshire to Essex, the horses on the large arable farms would be turned out into horse yards, or crew yards, which had food stores and open fronted shelters round the perimeter.

Though one yoke systems were worked throughout most of the year, in the seasons when the days were long and the pace of farm work moved at top speed, the two yoke system was worked.

The winter timetable for a two yoke farm would be: 5.30 a.m. feed water and muck out; 6.30 a.m. breakfast; 7 a.m. horses out to work; 12 p.m. back at the stables for a feed for the horses, and dinner for the horsemen; 1.30 p.m. horses back to the fields until 5 p.m. or darkness; horsemen to tea and then feed horses and finish stable work about 7 p.m.

They were long hours, but for many of the horsemen, the extra work mornings and evenings attending to the horses, was a love rather than a labour. In summertime, especially at haymaking and harvesting, the horses could be out at work in the fields until as late as 9 p.m. A good farmer would realise that the horses could only give so much, and they needed time to recover and be ready for the next day's spell of work, just as much as the farmer himself needed a good night's sleep. Mr. Dunlop, of Pett, remembers his father 'always insisted that the horses finished work by 8 p.m. during the harvest, so that they had a chance to get ready for the next day's work. Today, with the tractor, we just carry on until it is too dark to see.'

WORKING WITH HORSES ON THE ROAD

Even down to the beginning of the nineteenth century, pack-horses in strings of up to seventy, were used in some districts, so bad was the state of the roads.

Jack Tucker of Tiverton in Devon, recalls the state of the roads on the day he met his first motor car: 'When going to town we always had to go with a good set of harness, or people would notice. This was always kept covered up for a good day. One day, about 1910, I had to go to Stuckeridge for a load of lime. I had to be up at 2 a.m. to catch the horses. In those days we harnessed horses in line and you had to be careful to follow the routs (ruts) in the road. They would be up to 18 in deep and often the roadman had to walk ahead of you filling them in with stones. If you wanted to turn out of the routs, you had to fill in with stones first to get out—otherwise you could easily snap the shafts of the wagon. That was the day I saw my first car. It had brass rails like bullock's horns and lamps as big as dinner plates. When cars first came on the roads, a horse gazing over a gate, and seeing one coming in a cloud of dust, would take fright and gallop off round the field, and you'd have a job finding him.'

Working with the heavy horses on the roads, the horsemen chose the routes which avoided the worse hills, especially if laden. Ted Halliday, an ex-London horseman explained how they 'rested the horses five to ten minutes at the bottom of a hill before tackling it.

You had to study your own horse and judge what he could do. Where possible we snaked up the worse of the hills.' Harry Aldridge pointed out the dangers of going up a steep hill too close to the preceding cart: 'Never follow too close. Wait till the first horse is up before you start—in case he can't hold his load and starts to come back at you.'

Timber hauling was regarded as one of the hardest jobs of all for the horse. The timber men were reputed to be rough and tough, and the horses often had to work over long hauls every day.

All road vehicles had some system of braking when going down hills. The most common way was to stop a back wheel turning by passing a chain through the spokes or to run the wheel up on to an iron slipper. Each wagon carried its own slipper, but in the border counties of England and Wales, large slippers with two iron wheels were used by the timber hauliers on some of the steepest hills. Three or four of these were left at the side of the road at the top of each hill. If you used one to descend you left it by the side of the road ready for the next passing wagon to carry it to the top again.

But, as Jimmy Cheshire explained, 'Not everyone used their slipper and if you thought you could get down the hill by running the wagon's wheels against the side of the road, you did so—but you made a mess of the verge. You then had to look out for the lengthsman, because if he saw you, he'd come and swear at you for spoiling his work. But if, in using your slipper you dug up the road surface, you had the local bobby after you quick, 'cos it was against the law.'

THE WAGONER AND THE LAW

If your wagon's wheels were shod with strakes (short sections of iron nailed to the wooden rim) instead of iron tyres, you were breaking the law if you chained the wheel to descend a hill rather than using a slipper. This was because the straked wheels were rough and tore at the surface of the road. Bert Boulton explained how when picking up the slipper, 'when you got to the bottom, then you had to watch how you got hold of him (the slipper), he wor always a bit hot'.

In the towns, when you pulled up at the side of the road, you had to lock chain one wheel before you could leave the horse unattended. Alf Edwards, ex drayman at a Wolverhampton brewery recalled how some drivers returned to the brewery yard a little the worse for wear after a day's delivering. 'One day we watched one of the lads pull into the yard, his pair pulling hard at the traces. He went up to the foreman, a bit unsteady, and complained to him about the dray, suggesting it could do with a visit to the workshops, "T'would run better if the lock chain were off", the foreman growled at him. The driver's face went redder than ever. He had had so many free pints on his round that he hadn't noticed he'd travelled miles with the back wheel chained. For a long time he was not allowed to forget his mistake, for everywhere he went his dray went bump, bump, bump, where the tyre had been worn flat.'

Though carters could (and still can) be charged for being drunk in charge of a horse, the current rate being £6, no one could take away a licence, and so their livelihood.

Bill Corns took great delight in telling of another of the perks of being a wagoner: 'As the horse was not allowed to be left unattended, the wagoner had the distinction of being the only person who could legally urinate in the street—as long as he used the off side of his vehicle!'

The habit of riding on the shafts of a cart or wagon, though dangerous, was common enough on the farms. It was an offence to do so on the public highway and the local village policeman often had to warn the carters not to persist in the practice.

Horses very quickly learnt to walk on the left hand side of the road and none of them needed headlights to enable them to find their way home in the dark.

To make it easier for the law to identify wagons, an act was passed as far back as the reign of George III making it compulsory for the owner of every wagon to paint his name etc. 'in large letters upon some conspicuous part of such wagon'.

TALKING TO HORSES

Though many horsemen did swear at their charges, the best amongst them generally spoke to them in a gentle manner. Tommy Hirons, a seasoned wagoner from Shropshire, gave this advice: 'The quieter you handle a horse, the better he'll like you. Never shout at him, even if he's in the wrong.'

In each district the horsemen had their own special language for talking to the horses and giving their orders. Though a few of the commands, such as Woh, were universal, others were very localised and a horse brought up to the commands of one area would have to learn them all over again if it were sold to another part of the country.

There were as many commands to turn left and right as there were local dialects and an attempt is made to map these in the glossary.

The extent to which the horsemen talked to their horses varied considerably from one area to another. In some districts few words were spoken, the reins being used to give directions. Even when starting up, instead of the normal click of the tongue and a word of encouragement to the horses, the reins would be given a flick and the horse moved forward in answer to that command. One southern Scot remarked on the amount of talk used for working horses in the parts of England he had visited, 'here we use the reins and work our horses with far less noise'. However, another Scot, Stephens, in his *Encyclopedia of Agriculture* writes: 'Reins alone would be sufficient to control horses but the use of the voice breaks the monotony of both man and beast.'

At the other extreme were the wagoners and ploughmen who could control their horses practically by word of mouth alone. Horses readily learnt to obey voice commands and understood what was required of them. A good horseman could, with a little patience, soon teach a team to work to voice commands and rarely have to use reins, or lines.

Where teams were driven in line, although a boy was often used to lead the front horse, it was not uncommon to see the wagoner walking along beside three or four horses, and controlling them, not with reins, but by word of mouth and the occasional use of his whip. This meant having a trusted leader horse which would not only be relied upon to answer the commands of the wagoner, but could bring the rest of the team to follow suit. A bad leader would need the added expense of a boy to lead it.

To train a horse to working by voice meant talking to it all the time, and as Mr. Fisher, of Yorkshire, pointed out, 'it wasn't what you said, but how you said it. Different inflections of the voice meant different things to the horse.'

Many horsemen talked to their horses as though they were human beings and this is not surprising when one realises that they were their only company for hours on end. Some horses learnt quite lengthy vocabularies and inflections of the voice, and would be able to judge for themselves just how far forward, or how much to one side, they were required to move.

The last word goes to Mr. Tregear, still working horses on his small Cornish farm, 'a man that don't talk to his horses is no horseman'.

FEEDING THE HORSES

As we have seen, most wagoners lived for their horses. Their whole lives seemed to depend on their turning out the finest horses on the farm or in the district. They would go to great lengths to try and achieve this. No food was too good for their horses and many were the times that the feed bins were raided to get them extra rations.

Mr. Nagginton, retired blacksmith at the foot of the Wrekin, tells how 'The wagoners used to pinch the corn for their horses. Often they would come to me to try and persuade me to make a skeleton key for them, which would fit the cornloft door. Often too, they so overfed their horses that they would come and try to get me to bleed them. But I wouldn't do that without I'd got their gaffer's permission. I remember two local wagoners once got competing against each other over the condition of their horses, so much so that they both overfed and both horses finished up with wet fever in the feet.'

Another wagoner described how they used to steal the oats for their horses by boring holes in the granary floor from underneath, and using a cork to seal it up when not in use. 'Whenever we wanted extra oats, we just pulled out the cork and the oats fell through like water from a tap.'

Usually the feed would be damped down with water, but in many areas the liquid considered best for doing this was the liquid contents of the chamber pot! This was reckoned to act as a sort of medicine and was 'great for making the horse's coat shine'. What is more, the horses appeared to relish the mixture!

The normal morning feed for the horses was a mixture of crushed oats and chaff (chopped oat straw and hay). Usually this would be sieved to remove any dust. Bill Laker, one of the last of the trained horsemen in Lincolnshire, described the feeding routine: 'Feed for this area was cut oats—the whole oat sheaf being put through the chaff cutter—a few crushed oats, and sometimes beans were added in the morning and bran in the afternoon. Every feed was damped down with water and treacle from the slap tub. Feeds were little and often, two or three handfuls at a time. All the dust was sieved out in one heap and all long pieces of chaff picked out, because if left in, the horses wouldn't eat them. If the farmer could see a heap of dust on the floor, he knew we were doing our job.'

Although other concentrates like beans and bran and at one time in Worcestershire 'barley that had been sprouted by burying it in the muck heap', were fed to the horses, by far the best concentrate for them and for reasons not quite known, was oats. The oats were crushed to aid the horses digestion. The chaff, hay and straw, were the bulky foods which helped the horses to chew their rations more thoroughly.

Bait, the term applied to the horse's feed in many districts (pubs called the Baiting Houses were where the wagoners used to stop to give their horses their meal, and where they themselves could enjoy a pint and a bite), was always carried by the wagoners and carters for any lengthy journey on the roads.

Ted Halliday, who drove a delivery van in London for many years, always carried a 'bait snack' for the horses with 15 to 20 lb of food: 'We used the nose bags as a seat till it was needed. We loosed the bit, but left it in the horse's mouth. This way it took the horse longer to eat its bait and so kept its mind off the traffic.'

In many areas the horses were given a bran mash, instead of their normal feed, on a Saturday evening, as a mild laxative over the weeked. Again, different areas had different theories and different ways. Fred Jordan, in Shropshire, never gave his horses a bran mash, 'we gave them boiled linseed which was a very good thing'.

WAGONER'S CURES

Not only did feeding routines vary from area to area, but so did the cures given to the horses for their various ailments. Linseed oil was the cure-all amongst the carters in Sussex. Mr. Dunlop, of Pett, gave 'a warm bottle of linseed oil to the horse, whether he liked it or not'. Cold tea was regarded as the cure for all horse illnesses around Deeside and as far north as Banff.

But many of the cures resorted to would have been unnecessary with better management and better understanding of the horse's needs. Many of the horse's troubles arose from over-feeding and under-exercising them at weekends, or during times of enforced lay off through snow etc. Monday morning leg, or weeds, was a common enough complaint, especially towards the end of the horse era. The horse's leg, usually a hind one, would swell considerably. Said Mr. Mais, of Fife, 'to alleviate the problem, you had to get the horses out of the stable and exercise them'. A remedy for reducing the swelling, from further north, was to 'wind a straw rope round the affected leg and pour water over it. This had the effect of shrinking the rope and thus the swelling on the leg'.

Grease was another complaint, usually of the hind feet, caused by too rich food in relation to the amount of work given to the horses. Again the leg swelled, and could get so bad that the swollen area 'shook like jelly'. A greasy discharge oozed out of the affected parts and the accompanying smell was bad enough for horses suffering from grease to be known as 'stinkers'. Grease caused an itch, and an affected horse would stamp and fidget in his stable all night long. But it seldom prevented a horse from working; in fact, working the horse was one of the best remedies.

The wagoner's cure for grease, in Shropshire and many other

parts of the country, was to plaster the affected leg with 'closet manure and buckets of lime'. The ammonia in the closet manure was considered to be beneficial. 'It fairly dried up the grease in two or three days.'

Though most horsemen agree that grease was caused by 'giving the horse too much corn without having the work for it', dirt on the legs was also blamed. This was said to cause the itchiness in the first place. Said Bill West of Wadebridge, Cornwall: 'As dirt also causes grease, we walked the horse through the pond to loosen the dirt. It wasn't easy to clean, all the muck off even by brushing and combing. Once you've got the grease, it's very difficult to get rid of, so you have to be on the watch for it all the time.'

Mr. Wales, of the Fellsides on the Cumberland/Westmorland borders, gives the causes of grease as 'too rich a feed, too little work, and washing the horses with cold water when they are sweating. We put salts and sometimes sulphur, in the horse's feed on a Saturday night. But, as this opens up the horse's pores, you had to be careful not to let them get wet, or they would end up with a chill.'

Another cause of a chill was allowing a sweating horse to drink too much cold water, too quickly. To prevent this, Mr. Beard, 'when bringing the horses in from the field after work, always left the bit in the horse's mouth when letting him drink, as this slowed him up a bit.'

A horse which was required to stand all day in a market when brought straight from the fields, often developed hot feet. Harry Hodgkins, retired horse dealer, as a lad used to have to 'get a bucket of cow muck and put the horse's foot in it to draw out the heat, and keep the hoof cool. Another way was to cut up old brewer's hop sacks, wet them, and tie them round the horse's feet.'

For cracks in the feet, caused in summer by the hard ground, stockholm tar seems to have been a universal remedy.

Lameness was the most common complaint found amongst the heavy horses, but sores caused by ill-fitting harness or working in adverse weather conditions without protection, were not uncommon. Mr. Wales would 'wash all sores with cold water and salt for 20 minutes', but Bert Boulton always used 'hot water and salt'. Rubbing cow dung into a sore to dry it up was a common practice in some areas.

To dry up a badly bleeding cut, a handful of flour rubbed on to it often did the trick. Cobwebs were also used extensively to stop bleeding; there was usually an ample supply available at close quarters.

Bleeding a horse, was at one time a cure-all for most horse troubles.

A special knife known as a fleam, was used to puncture the vein. The fleam was placed on the vein and hit smartly by a blood stick. This practice died out some years ago, though local bleeding is still advocated for some ills and more than one horseman described how to bleed a horse by 'nicking the fourth or fifth ridge on the roof of the horse's mouth with a razor'.

Bleeding was practised 'to cool a horse down', but the opposite was recommended as an old cure for pneumonia. 'When the horse went down, you packed it round with dung. The dung heated up and helped to sweat out the fever in the horse.'

In those far-off days before antibiotics became the modern cure-all, there must have been more than a little good sense in the cures handed down from one generation of wagoners to another. But very few of their remedies are practised today on the few heavy horses left to fall ill. Antibiotics have brought us surer methods of curing ills, but have lost us many colourful and, no doubt successful remedies.

HORSE DEALERS AND COPERS

More malpractices seem to have been resorted to at horse markets than any other market where animals or commodities were bought and sold. The dealers seemed to revel in the fact that the onus was on the buyer to spot the faults and not on the seller to declare them. *Caveat emptor*—let the buyer beware—was the watchword of these markets.

It is worth recording just a few of the more common tricks resorted to by unscrupulous dealers. Many were told by the men themselves, now retired from the market through age, lack of horses or possibly because of the stricter checks kept on buying and selling. Some were masters at the art of faking or bishoping (after a man called Bishop who, in the eighteenth century had a reputation for making old horses look young).

As a horse's age can be told up to about ten years old, by examining its teeth, they could make a three year old look a four or five year old by knocking out the side milk teeth, or make an old horse look younger by filing down the teeth to resemble those of a younger animal.

Another common practice for making an old horse look younger was to colour it up. 'A black horse, going grey around the temples and legs, responded well to touching up with sticks of black indian ink. Many a man has bought a black horse at the fair one day, and found he'd bought a grey the next! An old grey one needed a ball of whitening rubbing into its coat.'

To get rid of the tell tale hollows above the eyes, 'blow up the ogles. Pierce them first with a pin, put your mouth to the hole and blow. They will stay like that for a few days and the horse will look much younger. Also, pull out some of the hair from the legs to show up the hooves.'

'If you are selling a horse that is lame in one foot, take the shoe off the other foot to make it just, and only just, as tender as the lame one. The horse then won't know which one to go lame on!'

'To make a horse go well, a drop of turps on the frog of the foot dried it up and made the horse lift his feet and prance,'—in pain?

Having sold the horse, the dealer would not be too keen to have it brought back and most of the large marts allowed a few days to return horses if not satisfied. For the Emporium in Birmingham, the deadline for returning horses sold at the Thursday fair was mid-day on Saturday. Mr. Beard recalls the delaying tactics that used to go on to prevent the horses arriving back before mid-day: 'On a Saturday morning the roads leading to the Emporium would be strategically patrolled by employees of those not wishing to have the horses returned. They kept a look out for anyone likely to be on their way to return a horse and would pretend to want to buy it. They then took as long as they could haggling with bogus offers, buying drinks in pubs, and asking to see the horses going through their paces, till finally, when mid-day arrived, they could just disappear.'

The retired dealers were also forthcoming in telling what they themselves looked for when buying a horse. For Teddy Stephens of Wolverhampton, there were three important things to look out for: 'First try the horse's lamps, to check for blindness, secondly feel for ringbone and lastly, give the horse the whip and if he roars like a bull he is broken winded.'

Mr. Naggington offered this advice: 'If you are buying a horse, make sure you see it trotted back and forth on hard ground. Soft ground can hide a lot of sins. Make sure too, that the person is holding the halter rope at least 18 in away from the horse; by holding it tight to the horse a knowing person can stop a horse's head from nodding, which is a sign of lameness.'

For most people, the feet were the most important part to be examined. Even 2000 years ago Xenophon wrote: 'In examining a horse look first to the legs, and in examining the legs look first to the feet.'

Not all dealers were dishonest, but the trade had more than its fair share of rogues. There was one Midlands dealer who repeatedly boasted to his prospective buyers: 'I'm the most honest horse dealer you'll ever meet. I'll tell you all the horse's faults—once the money's in my pocket!'

Many less rational ways of judging the qualities of a horse were used by the old horsemen. A common Midlands jingle repeated by Mr. Griffiths from Kinlet in Shropshire goes:

> One white leg, try him,
> Two white legs, buy him,
> Three white legs, doubt him,
> Four white legs, do without him.

Another very old saying heard throughout the country was:

> No good horse ever was a bad colour,
> And no bad horse ever was a good colour.

But, for Harry Hodgkins, 'a wall-eyed horse was always a dodgy one', whilst 'horses with roman noses and those with rat tails were always good uns' for Alf Edwards.

Many horses appeared to have a well developed sense of humour, as many a wagoner recalled from experience. The wagoners themselves liked a bit of fun too. The following incident happened to a Shropshire wagoner and was related by Mike Mantle.

'The wagoner liked his pint and was often known to stay at the local pub till long after dark, leaving his poor horse to wait patiently in the yard outside. The wagoner would rely on the horse taking him home whilst he slept off the effects of the evening in the back of the wagon. One evening some of the local lads slipped out of the bar early, and after a while the yard gate was heard being closed. Others in the bar kept the wagoner liberally supplied with drinks till an hour later he stumbled out into the yard and climbed slowly up into the wagon. Giving the horse a cursory command to take him home, he flopped down into the body of the vehicle, but was soon up again when the horse had not moved and the yard was full of folks holding their sides laughing. It was some few minutes before the bewildered wagoner regained enough of his senses to see why his horse was refusing to move. In the dark the local lads had unyoked the horse, pulled the shafts through the bars of the gate and shut it. The horse was then yoked up again to the shafts, on the other side of the gate to the rest of the wagon.

Though the laughter has long since died away over the Shropshire hills, the tale, and many more like it, have remained. But the numbers of old horsemen, wagoners, carters and ploughmen grow smaller every day, much to the detriment of the traditions and colour of our society.

CHAPTER NINE

Decorating
The Heavy Horse Harness

EARLY DECORATIONS

Ever since he learned to harness the horse, man seems also to have felt the need to decorate the harness in one way or another. The two main reasons for decorating which have been put forward are, first the desire by the owner to show off, not only the qualities of his horse but also the extent of his own wealth. This is made evident in early drawings and paintings showing horses covered in elaborate trappings of silk, gold and other ornate materials. These would all have belonged to a wealthy class of horse owner and were mostly confined to the ridden horse as this was the only practical way to travel. The ordinary layman, if he could afford a horse and harness, could certainly not afford to decorate it in such an elaborate fashion. All the harness decorations that have been unearthed prior to the eighteenth century would appear to have belonged, if not to ·kings and princes, then certainly men of substance.

The second reason for decorating harness was brought about very early in history, because of man's fear of the unknown. Until quite recent times superstition played an important part in man's everyday behaviour. There developed a need in man to protect himself and his property from these unknown influences, and the way he invented of doing this was by hanging charms or amulets on whatever was to be protected. Charms were given the power of holding the unknown at bay. They have been traced back to very early man and are still worn today for the power which people believe them to possess.

As far as decorating horse harness is concerned, to protect the horse from the unknown, many different charms have been worn at different times in history. Most persistent through the years has been the charm, usually a bright object, worn to protect the horse from the influence of the evil eye. It was believed that evil could be conveyed from the eyes of envious or angry persons, to infect those gazed upon, unless the evil could be reflected back again by a shiny surface or some other charm. Domestic animals were believed to be in special danger and needed most protection. Of the modern nations, parts of southern Italy were probably the last to harbour these superstitions. Horns, pieces of wolf skin and crescent shaped amulets were extensively worn on horse trappings in the firm belief that they would ward off the evil eye. That these superstitions go back a long way is emphasised by the fact that Christianity had very little influence on the choice of objects in use as charms.

Where Christianity did have an influence on decoration found on horse trappings was through the practice of displaying armorial bearings, crests, coats of arms etc. Many of the symbols used in heraldry are of Christian origin. Embroidered saddle cloths for the riding horse of the wealthy gave way to chased models of the family crests worn on the harness of the carriage horses, when improved road conditions made these vehicles popular in the eighteenth century. Up to this point in history we have seen that the heavy horse in harness had been relatively little used, and certainly there was little incentive for wealthy owners to lavish money on trappings for its crude and heavy harness.

The earliest decorations seen on the heavy harness in the middle of the eighteenth century were of three types. First, a simple decoration was achieved by using leather thonging. A full faced bridle in the Museum of Leathercraft, at Walsall, is dated 1744 and it has considerable decoration of this sort. The initials T.C. are worked into the blinkers as though they were embroidered. The second method of decorating was by tooling the leather to bring out a design. A correspondent to *Saddlery and Harness* in 1903 wrote of a housen he had picked up at a local farm 'with the date 1769, raced in, also T.H. and a floral design in the corners and round the edges'. A similar housen is in Hereford Museum, dated 1789. This practice of dating the harness was carried on in some districts into the present century, many bridles found in the Lincolnshire part of the country have their date of manufacture displayed on the browband.

But the third, and most noticeable form of decoration seen at this time was a woollen fringe around the housen, usually of two or three colours, both red and blue, and red and yellow being popular. Sometimes woollen tassels were attached to other parts of the harness, especially the reins.

Tassels and fringes continue to decorate harness at shows in some parts of Great Britain. The fancy stitching is also still used on parts of the harness, though not in leather thonging. However, apart from the blocking of the blinkers and the creasing of the edges of straps, no fancy tooling is done today.

The first signs of the use of brass ornamentation on heavy horse harness was towards the end of the eighteenth century. Apart from buckles, brass appears as oval decorations in the middle of the blinkers, and soon after, on a face piece, and on the corners of the cart saddle housings. It is significant that these positions on the harness were the very places where the gentry of the day were displaying their silver chased crests and monograms on the grand harness of the carriage horse. There are many pictures by Pyne in his *Microcosm*, at the beginning of the nineteenth century, of horses in harness, but only a very few show brass decorations on blinkers and saddles. Not a single face piece is depicted in any of these drawings.

There can be no doubt that the wagoners of that time were decorating their harness in a way that mimicked the silver chasing on the carriage horse harness. There are no signs to suggest that in fact they had been influenced by fears of the evil eye. We know of no charms being carried by these horses to ward off evil influences prior to the wearing of brass decorations. As the brass decorations first appeared on the blinkers, we can only assume that the wagoners were more influenced by a desire to mimic their masters' show of opulence than to start a fashion for warding off an evil influence they had not feared before.

Because a similar brass decoration appeared on a face piece on the horse's forehead, many writers have believed this to be a sun flash consciously put there by the wagoner to ward off evil spirits, but there is no firm evidence to suggest this to be correct. Carriage horses wore face pieces long before their heavyweight brothers, and the only decorations worn there were the crests of the different owners.

DEVELOPMENT OF HORSE BRASSES

We now have to look for other reasons than that of warding off evil spirits, for the wagoners developing a taste for hanging brasses of varying shapes all over their horses' harness. The practice started quietly enough and only reached its peak in the fifty years from 1870 to 1920; but the puzzle as to who started the fashion and at what moment in time remains unsolved. Many theories have been put forward and many dates given, but what is remarkable is that although brasses designed to hang from a loop of leather were in existence long before the middle of the nineteenth century, they were not depicted by the artists of the day. Even the Herrings, who were great lovers of painting horses in their harness down to the smallest detail, fail to show any horse brasses hung on the leather. Certainly they show plenty of blinker and saddle brasses, and the housens are all gaily fringed with coloured worsted, but there are no pendant type horse brasses.

Evidence has been put forward of dated brasses as early as 1760, but as one can never be sure that the date displayed on an object is in fact its date of manufacture, it is tempting to dismiss these if they occur well before the practice became commonplace. There are many dated horse brasses in existence, but these do not appear in any numbers until the 1850s. The earliest examples include; 1776 at Salisbury Museum and currently misplaced; 1830, Birmingham City Museum; 1837, Bristol Museum. As any fashion takes time to gain momentum we can safely assume that the mode for wearing horse brasses with hangers attached started in this country around the end of the eighteenth century, but was of little significance for the average wagoner until about fifty years later.

As to who started the fashion, if we take a close look at the patterns of the earliest hand-made brasses we find a preponderance of heart, crescent, star and sunflash designs. These strongly suggest a gipsy influence. The first gipsies came to Britain by way of Europe in the early fifteenth century, and to this day are amongst the most superstitious members of the community. It is quite probable that they believed in the power of the evil eye and that newcomers to this country from southern Europe in the late eighteenth century brought the fashion of wearing these brasses with them. Indications are that these amulets have an earlier history in southern Europe than this country. Certainly the gipsies had the skills to work the brass sheets, and it is believed that most of the hand-made brasses were fashioned by them.

The wagoners of the day would have seen this type of hanging brass as a decoration worth having for their own horses. There is no reason to believe that they saw them in the light of charms. Though many wagoners enjoying their twilight years know of the symbolic meanings given to the various designs of horse brasses by twentieth-century writers, none of them remember either themselves, their fellow wagoners, or their fathers before them, regarding the brasses as anything but decorations. From his conversations with horsemen in East Anglia, Ewart Evans in *The Horse in the Furrow*, 1960, comes to the same conclusion. Richards, in *Horse Brass Collections*, 1945, quotes a letter from a Kentish saddler: 'I have never heard of any such claims for the potency, or for the ancient origin of horse brasses. I have been selling them now for over sixty years, and sixty years ago was selling them to carters then sixty years of age and over. They were always chosen either for their prettiness—a matter of taste—or for their easiness to clean.'

As soon as manufacturers found that there was a growing market for these 'hanging pieces', then the door was wide open for the introduction of all sorts of designs. By 1825, when the casting of horse brasses seems to have got under way, the manufacturers were already engaged in the production of a wide range of the simpler brass decorations fitted with short pieces of wire to pin them to the blinkers, cart saddles, and anywhere else on the harness the wagoners chose to wear them.

Their first designs of hanging brasses were similar to the simple patterns of the handmade ones and, whether as a result of requests from wagoners, or as is more likely, because they could see the sales opportunities, the manufacturers began producing brasses of the most intricate designs. Not only were the designs geometrical patterns, but many heraldic devices and emblems associated with the various trades were amongst the earliest to be produced. Many writers have attributed the production of the heraldic designs to orders from large estates. A more feasible explanation is that, as the manufacturers also produced the crests and monograms for the carriage harness, and employed chasers to produce these miniature works of art, it was a short step to insert these heraldic devices into a frame which could be hung on the leather instead of being fixed with studs. The manufacturers had books of specimen crests with hundreds of designs from which to chose their patterns. Often deliberate alterations were made to well known crests to avoid objections from their owners, but it all added up to the fact that the wagoners could now imitate their 'betters' by displaying their own range of heraldic designs.

Apart from those made for municipal authorities, horse brasses with crests or coats of arms produced specially for private individuals are very rare indeed.

The manufacture of the brasses and the patterns produced will be explored in the following chapter. We will return now to the ways they were used by the wagoners to decorate the harness.

WEARING THE BRASS DECORATIONS

There is no difficulty in finding places on the harness to decorate with the ovals, octagons and other shapes originally produced to display on the blinkers and saddle housings. They appear on the housens, on the collar side-pieces, on the loin and hip straps and even on the breech band. Small versions are used to decorate reins and other narrow straps. They are easy to attach as the only tool needed is a sharp point to bore holes in the leather to take the wire pins fixed to the back of the brass.

However, in order to show off the new hanging pieces, a whole new range of special straps was needed. The first to appear was the face piece, a broad strap hanging down on the horse's forehead.

For this reason, although some of the trade catalogues described the new brasses as hanging pieces, most referred to them as face pieces, and, in the earliest catalogue by Newton, as face drops. At first the brasses were probably mounted separately onto a piece of leather and then strapped to the brow-band of the bridle. This type of face piece is still used today over many parts of the country. It is either buckled through a hole cut in the brow-band or kept in place by cutting a small piece out of the top of the brow-band. They can be taken off at will and kept for special occasions. Many Midland bridles, and especially bridles used for town work, were later constructed with a built-in face piece, usually large enough to take two and very occasionally three horse brasses.

In Scotland, face pieces were not often worn. In fact, the straps developed to carry the horse brasses in England were rarely seen north of the border where a completely different set of straps, with a different type of decoration was developed. James Horsborough, of Fife, who called the face pieces 'facens', explained how they were only occasionally worn in those parts, but were 'no a guid thing as they rub all the hair off under them and begin to skin the horses'.

The next strap to appear decorated with horse brasses was the

The Lancashire style of harness decoration with real flowers carried in small brass vases. Note too the long runners covered with heart-shaped tips, and the wearing of a hemp halter under the bridle. This is one of the Shires worked by Thwaites Brewery of Blackburn. (*Thwaites, Blackburn*)

strap joining the collar and the girth of the saddle between the
front legs of the horse. This strap is often referred to as a 'martingale',
but a truer description is that of breastplate or breaststrap. A true
martingale connects the horse's bit or reins to the girth and is only
seen on riding and light driving harness. It prevents the horse
throwing its head up. The breastplate of the heavy horse harness,
if it were worn for any other reason than to carry decorations,
helped to keep the collar from riding upwards or the girth from slipping backwards. Explained Willie Gaw of Wigtownshire, 'It kept
the girth forrart. You would wear it on a horse that's kinna pish-
mither waisted' (ant waisted). A similar strap was worn on some

Fig 35
The English Harness
Decorations

a. facepiece.
b. breastplate.
c. fly head terret.

d. neck strap.
e. hameplate.
f. rein hanger.

g. harness bells
h. side strap
i. leading rein.

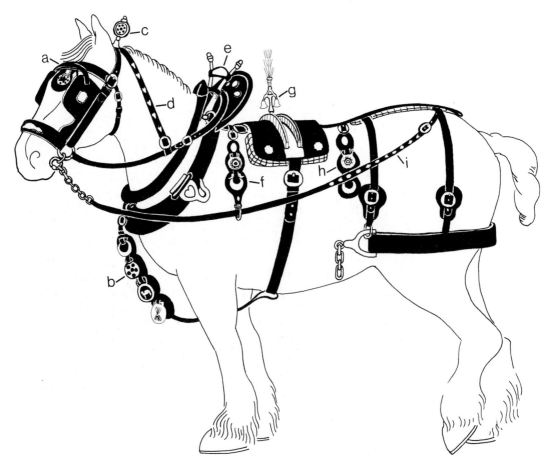

carriage harness and was then known as a false martingale. It was the custom to display crests on the false martingale and this in turn led to the development of the large brass covered breastplates which some heavy horses had to wear in the cause of decoration.

In its simplest form the breastplate is a plain strap with loops and buckles either end. The easiest way to hang the brasses is to sew them on with loops of leather. A similar shaped piece of leather to that of the brass can be sewn on with it as a backing. Three or four brasses can be sewn on in this manner so that they overlap slightly. Breastplates of this simple style are often found in the south eastern counties, especially parts of Kent.

To begin with the carters probably made up their own decorative breastplates. Breastplates made from old pieces of breech bands and back bands from plough harness are often seen to this day. Stitching was crude and often copper rivets intended for repairing the machine belting or binder canvasses replaced the stitching. Although carters continued to make up their own straps, the greater part of the breastplates came from the saddler's shop. A carter may have taken in to the saddler a number of brasses which he wanted making up into a breastplate, but on the whole they were sold with the brasses of the saddler's choice already in position. Not only did the saddlers make them up, but later still some manufacturers produced breastplates and included them in their catalogues.

The standard pattern of breastplate consists of a strap with a loop and buckle at the top, broadening into a piece of leather wider than the widest brass to be hung on it, then narrowing again to a strap with a second loop and buckle to go round the girth. Sometimes the leather of the main body of the breastplate is swelled to coincide with the brasses and a pattern is often punched around the edges of the leather. The breastplate usually carries three to five brasses. Any more than five on this pattern would be a waste from the decorative point of view because of the limited length of the breastplate on view.

In some of the northern counties broad breastplates with double hanging straps to attach them to the hames were occasionally made large enough to take a row of three brasses on top, followed by two underneath and a single one at the bottom. On the whole, however, the further north one goes the smaller the breastplate becomes, until in Scotland they were seldom worn with more than a single brass. In these parts too, the bottom strap to the girth was not always worn, though an attachment at the back was often provided to take one. In Westmorland and Cumberland the fashion was to wear a small medallion attached by a strap through a hole punched in the bottom of the collar.

Breastplates carrying as many as ten brasses were found in the south, but these cumbersome monsters were more of a hinderance than a decoration.

The practice of trimming the edges of the breastplates with small brass studs was popular in parts of Shropshire, Cheshire and north Wales, whilst along the south coast, from Hampshire to Devon the larger twelve pointed stars, known as one inch tips in the trade, were used for the same purpose.

One inch tips were made in at least twelve different shapes including hearts, ovals, crescents, shields, stars, octagons, diamonds and others. They are still being made in Walsall today by the old established firm of W. Thacker & Co., but more find their way to the fancy goods trade than to the harness. As they were simple to attach they were used on all parts of the harness but are mostly associated with the decorated reins. The leading rein in particular was brassed up to within 18 in of the bit, the plain section being left for the wagoner to catch hold of. The driving reins were never decorated, nor was the bearing rein, but a decorated strap from the top of the bridle to the bearing rein, on the near side of the horse, and usually called a necklace, was popular amongst the wagoners in many parts of the country.

Many patterns of side straps, called variously runners, hip straps, loin straps, rein hangers, flyers etc., were made up to decorate the horse from the side view. They were all attached either to the meeter straps or to the crupper, and hung down either side of the horse with two to four horse brasses displayed on each. Rein hangers, designed to hold the reins up, are provided with a metal loop at the bottom, through which the reins pass.

Two other forms of decorated strap are found in south east England. The first is the tail strap seen in parts of Kent and Sussex. It was worn about 4 in from the base of the dock—usually when tails were plaited up when ploughing during winter. At the other end of the horse, crossed face straps were fitted over the nose between the brow-band and nose-band. This style of decoration was more often seen in Europe and America, but was only found in this country on rare occasions.

THE SCOTTISH DECORATIONS

The Scottish ploughmen never took to the horse brass in the same way that their counterparts south of the border did. Up to the present day the Scottish horsemen lavished more care and attention on the leather of the harness than on any form of decoration. Stephens, a Scot, writing in 1849, did not approve of ornamentation for horse harness on farms. 'It looks best when left plain, of the best material and workmanship. Brass or plated buckles and brow-bands, worsted rosettes, and broad bands of leather tattooed with filigree sewing, serve only to load and cover the horse when at work, to create trouble, collect dirt, and at best display a wasteful and vulgar taste in the owner. Whatever temptation there may be in the towns to show off the grandeur of the teams of rival establishments, such displays of vanity are incompatible with the country.'

The special decorated straps that were used in Scotland were

Fig 36	a. kidney strap.	c. side flash	e. false buckle	g. neck leather
The Scottish Show Straps	b. rein hanger	d. rump strap	f. breast plate	h. fly head terret

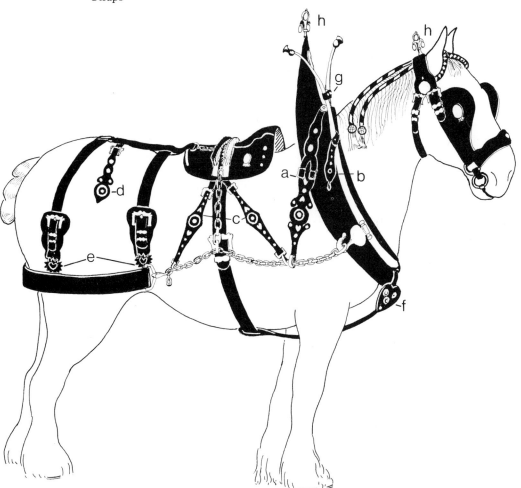

designed to keep the harness in position when the horses were paraded in the show ring (Fig. 36). The kidney strap, or neckplate, was coupled either side of the collar and clipped into the draught chains. Side flashes were clipped into the same link of the draught chain and buckled into the civet ring of the saddle. Rein hangers were hung on to the hames in front of the kidney straps, collar or back straps decorated the back of the peak of the high collar and the rump strap was buckled to the ring of the crupper. Decorated false buckles and other strap ornaments were used on the hame strap.

Although the first Scottish show straps had brass decorations, when the nickel fittings became available, they were preferred by the Scottish ploughmen. Said James Horsborough of Fife, 'The silver decorations were easier kept. The brass went green too quickly.' In England nickel decorations are usually associated with coastal areas, where the salt laden air tarnished the brass too quickly. In Scotland the nickel decorations and fittings stood up to the rigours of the weather better, and they also blended well with the high polish of the harness and the burnished hames and chains. Face pieces were never popular because a substantial brow-band needed to support it was not usually found on the Scottish bridles.

The actual decorations fixed to the straps were usually made in Walsall specially for the Scottish market. Thistle patterns were naturally popular, but the origin of the combination circle and knob so often found on the blinkers and show straps is difficult to trace. The bridle also had decorations on the cheek-strap, and a shield bearing the saddler's name was often displayed here. The saddle had small stud decorations; no large ovals, etc. as were found in the south. Also long plates on the back edge of the saddle kept the crupper straps from marring the saddle housing. The hip and loin straps were fitted with three or four studs each, but the finest decorations here were the large buckles so favoured by the Scots. Many patterns of buckle, including the Fluted, Clydesdale, Jenny Lind and many others were produced specially for the Scottish harness. The use of double metal keepers below the buckles to take the strap ends also enhanced this fine harness.

But of all the harness pieces worn in Scotland, the one which was most decorated was the ploughband. Enormous buckles to take the 4 in wide strap, decorated the near side of many of these ploughbands, as well as a host of other decorations with such designs as thistles or Speed the Plough.

In recent years all the decorated show straps, except the breast-plate, have lost favour with the horsemen still showing horses in harness in the ring. The use of meeter straps between the saddle and the collar eliminates the need for kidney and side straps. At the 1971 Highland Show, only one of the fifteen entrants decorated his harness with these straps.

THE SCOTTISH WOOLLEN DECORATIONS

The wool and floral decorations now used to display the harness in Scotland are of relatively recent origin. They are a modern folk art which appears to have developed from the displays of flowers and ribbons used to decorate the harness on special occasions just prior to the First World War. At first the plaiting and ribbons were used to decorate the horses' manes and tails, but later they were applied to the harness. Wire frames to carry the decorations on the saddle and britchen became known as the bridge and crown, and the designs acquired a standardisation not only for type of fittings but also for materials used.

The two classes now judged at the shows are for floral and woollen designs. The woollen class is the oldest and carries on the traditional

A pair of Clydesdales which won the best turn-out at the Scottish ploughing championships for Wm. Copeland. The small floral decorations are typical of the style used since the 1940's, and are still being made in the homes of farm workers. (*J. G. Wilson*)

pom-pom and ribbon display, but are more easily spoiled by the weather. The floral class, using first paper flowers, then milliner's sprays and finally the modern plastic flowers, last longer and display more colour. The traditional colours of blue and white are used for the diamond roll plait covering the wire frames and also for the ribbons and pom-poms of the woollen class.

A complete set of decorations, laboriously made up by the ploughman and his family, consists of the bridge over the saddle, the crown on top of the britchen, and the wee crown on top of the peaked collar, as well as smaller sprays for the forelook, top of the bridle, nine for the mane, two hame pieces, four britchen buckle decorations and three tails. Each district had its own distinctive style but the judges at the shows were looking for overall neatness. This involved designing the decorations so that the tops of the wee crown, bridge, crown and tails were all in a straight line.

The work of making the decorations could take two or three months of winter evenings. The small floral sprays were matched

Floral decorations on Scottish cart harness. Apart from the breast-plate, the decorated straps have mostly been discarded from Scottish show harness.
(William Copeland)

for colours and as many as fifty were needed to decorate a large bridge. Some ploughmen were specialists in the art. Men like William Copeland and Geordie Wilson became as famed for their work as did the saddlers whose harness they decorated. Turning out an average of two complete sets each winter they dominated the field in recent shows, both local and national. Horses decorated with floral displays by William Copeland won the first five places at the Royal Highland Show in 1970, and in the following year five of the first six in the woollen decorated class were wearing decorations made by the hands of Geordie Wilson. Both these men, like so many before them, worked for the pride of seeing their handicraft displayed on the horses and being judged in front of thousands of admirers of the heavy horse.

The ploughman and their families made up their own decorations. Some, like William Copeland, were so good at the art that their work was highly sought after by other ploughmen. (*David Gowans*)

OCCASIONS FOR WEARING THE DECORATIONS

Some of the decorations were permanent fixtures on the everyday

harness, both on the farms and in the cities. Particularly in the cities, many horsemen regarded all the decorations as part of the harness to be cleaned and worn every day. To them a horse was as undressed without its brassed up breastplate as it was without its collar. The pride these men took in their show of brass was akin to the pride taken by the drivers of the old steam engines who were never without a polishing rag in their hands. It usually worked out that the dirtier the job which the horseman was involved in, the more brass he used to adorn his horse, as if in an attempt to take folks eyes away from the contents of the carts. The coal merchant's horse and particularly the horses pulling the dustcarts were traditionally more brassed up than any others.

However, most decorations were kept wrapped up in chests only to see the light of day for special occasions. For the wagoner off the farm a special occasion could be a visit to market or to the station to fetch a load of feed or fertiliser, and hours would be spent the previous night polishing the brasses and rubbing up the harness ready for the journey. The desire to show off the horses came, not only from the wagoner walking proudly alongside his team, but also from the farmer, content to stay at home but knowing that his well turned out horses would be seen by the neighbours and suggest to them that here were the horses of a prosperous farmer.

In Scotland the regulation dress for going to town was different. As Jimmy Mathieson, who did a lot of carting fodder from the farm into Edinburgh, was told by his boss, 'For the love of God put on the clear hames and chains or the folk will no ken who the yokes belong to.' The normal farm hames were painted black but a shining steel set was specially kept, together with a set of chains kept bright by burnishing and stored in a bucket of lime for the day they were needed. A peaked collar with the special long hames would also be worn, and all the leather of the harness polished like glass. Few brass or nickel decorations were used by the Scottish horsemen on these occasions.

The ploughing matches were the occasions when the Scots 'went to town' on their harness decoration. As mentioned earlier, the decorated plough bands were the pride and joy of their owners. These ploughing matches became very popular amongst the Scottish ploughmen before the middle of the last century, and naturally the men engaged in competition not only wanted to show off their own ploughing skills, but also to show off the horses they were using.

As the practice of decorating the harness developed at ploughing matches all over Britain, so prizes were awarded for the best dressed teams. Many a proud, local harness-maker donated a matching pair of breastplates to be awarded to the best dressed horses, and as these would carry the name and address of his shop, he achieved a subtle form of advertising in return.

Another great ploughing occasion in parts of Scotland and the north of England, which called for some decoration of the horses, was the boon day, or ploughing day, for a new farmer. Mr. Wales of Westmorland explained how 'a new neighbour would take over a farm on Candlemas day, the second of February, and he would be faced with all his ploughing still to do. All the neighbours would get together and give him a boon day, a day's ploughing. All the ploughmen would compete with each other to see who could put up the best show, both at the ploughing and in the decoration of their horses. The day's work would cover most of the new farmer's oustanding ploughing and it would finish with a big dinner in the farm kitchen that evening. Boon days unfortunately went out with the coming of the tractor.'

Down in the south of England it was the harvest festival which provided the opportunity for decorating the horses and also the wagons. Complete turn-outs were judged on these occasions and it was a matter of great pride to a farm that their horse and wagon should be judged the best on show.

Sunday school outings in the country districts at one time involved the use of wagons to transport the children. This would call for decorations to suit the occasion and often competitions were held to find the best decorated wagon, which was given the honour of leading the procession. The above outing was photographed in Lincs. c.1908. (M.E.R.L)

Before the coming of the motor coach, Sunday school outings all over Great Britain were occasions for farmers lending their horses and wagons to take the children on an annual picnic. Usually this developed into a competition amongst the wagoners to put up the best show and in many areas judging took place and the winner had the honour of leading the convoy to the station or to the picnic site.

May-day provided the occasion for the town horses and their handlers to be judged annually. Most of the big cities in England followed this tradition. The day would start with the horses being dressed and judged in their own stable yards for the best turned out horse of that yard. Later in the day many cities held May-day parades in which the dressed horses and their vehicles took part for further judging. In Liverpool, Manchester and the Midlands cities particularly, May-day was a great occasion for decorating the heavy horses.

In London the May-day tradition died out and was replaced by the London Cart Horse Parade on Whit Monday round the inner circle of Regents Park. The event, started in 1886, became very popular indeed and backed by the R.S.P.C.A. did great work in improving the standard of horsemanship applied to the heavy cart horses. The judges were not concerned with the points of the horse, but 'prizes will be awarded to drivers whose horses show exceptionally good treatment and whose harness is approved and shows reasonable wear and cleanliness, and that it fits and is connected to the vehicle properly'.

Describing the display of decorations in 1902 a correspondent to *Saddlery and Harness* writes: 'Most were excellent but a few were decidedly vulgar—especially those with huge satin rosettes hiding half the head and others fixed to hip and loin straps. This may be a fair exhibition of millinery skill, but would look better on the prize ox in a butcher's shop at Christmas. Neck straps and the back ends of leading reins widened out to 3 or 4 in with coloured woollen edging completely mar the symmetry of a handsome horse, yet who could have the heart to condemn such a labour of love? A prize for the best decorated horse without its natural beauty hidden would be a good thing.'

Another correspondent in 1911 describes how 'the majority of turn-outs vied with each other in presenting an attractive appeara-ance, vivid touches of colour and brightness being given by the decorations and the highly polished brasses lavishly used on almost every horse'. This was the heyday of the use of brasses for the decoration of the heavy horse.

Special brasses were awarded by the Cart Horse Society and carters were very keen to gain one as this represented to them a hallmark of perfection.

The Van Horse Society, formed in 1904 for lighter delivery horses, held a similar parade each Easter Monday. In 1966 the two societies were amalgamated and a joint parade is still held every Easter Monday. Here can be seen, paraded in front of thousands of onlookers, the finest display of heavy horses in harness still to be found in Great Britain.

A different form of competition were the special classes for decorated horses in harness at the local and national agricultural shows. Here the competition was very keen and exacting. These were the occasions which brought out the secret formulas for polishing the harness (boot polish mixed with whisky, for one keen Scots showman) and also the sets of harness kept specially, and often made specially, for these shows. Hours and days of polishing and preparation of the harness and decorations were needed to achieve the necessary perfection to win these classes. It is encouraging to see a revival of this colourful tradition at many of our agricultural shows. The art of decorating the heavy horse harness is far from being dead.

CHAPTER TEN

Horse Brasses

METHODS OF MANUFACTURE

The first horse brasses were made by hand from hammered sheets of brass known as latten. Using this latten brass, the early makers of horse brasses worked out patterns of their choice and cut, filed and hammered the brass to get the shape.

The early patterns were simple ones with little or no working of the brass, other than the bare outline. Often a hammer was used to raise the centre slightly, and the hammer marks show quite clearly on the back, but on the whole the designs were simple and small.

Handmade brasses continued to be made long after the first cast ones appeared about 1825. As we have seen in the previous chapter, the earliest handmade brasses were most likely made by the gipsies, but as the demand for them grew, specialist workers in metal, working in town workshops, produced a number of finely made brasses. Patterns made to order from these skilled artisans were still being occasionally produced as late as 1900. The 'Bosville Arms', at Rudstone in Yorkshire, has a pair of breastplates and matching face pieces with brasses all fashioned to resemble plough-shares. They are part of a set specially handmade for a champion ploughman from Lincolnshire about the turn of the century. Whatever their age, surviving handmade horse brasses are very rare indeed.

Once the manufacturers saw the potential of the horse brasses and started to cast them very cheaply, they rapidly took over their supply. Walsall in particular had many small brass foundries already casting brass buckles and other harness fittings and decorations. All they would need to produce the new hanging pieces was a pattern. There must have been a ready supply of pattern makers in the area designing the other fittings, as well as skilled chasers of the finer metal decorations. These men between them, produced the myriad of designs which came from the brass foundries in the next hundred years. At first they copied the simple designs of the early handmade brasses, then slowly their designs became more elaborate, and the readily available heraldic devices were introduced. Standard designs of frame were introduced to surround these borrowed crests and different combinations of frame and crest were produced.

The close community of manufacturers also 'borrowed' each other's designs, sometimes making a slight alteration in a com-

(opposite and overleaf) Front and back views of brasses: *top*, a hand made brass with hammer marks on the back; *middle left*, a cast brass with the sand marks on the unpolished back; *middle right*, an early stamped brass, a single punch being used to create a pattern from a stamped out blank; *bottom*, a later machine stamped brass, stamped out in one operation. *(Ratcliffe Photographs)*

petitor's design. At least nine different manufacturers who produced a catalogue of their patterns show the horseshoe with a horse's head inside, all with slight variations. There must have been at least the same number again being produced by small manufacturers who did not produce a catalogue. The so called flaming heart design also appeared in at least nine catalogues, though the variations in design were not always apparent. All the manufacturers seem to have included the plain crescent in their list.

The copying of each other's successful designs seems to have been fair game, but many manufacturers did make use of the diamond shaped registration mark between 1842 and 1883 to protect their designs. Very occasionally this mark can be found on the backs of brasses. After 1883 some new patterns appeared with 'Registered' cast into the front or back. Firms like William Overton and R. E. Thacker continued to produce and register new designs up to the First World War. After that date, apart from an occasional royalty brass, no new designs were produced specifically for the harness trade. This was the period when the souvenir brass began to take over the trade. There have probably since been as many designs of souvenir brasses produced as there were designs made specifically for the decoration of the horse harness.

The early pattern makers worked in wood—pear wood, and also soft metals, like lead and pewter, which could easily be moulded and chased. Many of these patterns still survive. Stanley Bros. of Walsall, established in 1832, and one of the few remaining manufacturers of harness furniture in the country, have hundreds of them in their pattern store. Here new patterns are still being designed for the souvenir trade, but the method of producing the first model has altered somewhat, they are now designed in plasticine on the back of a dinner plate!

To return to the casting of the brasses, the above firm, like one or two smaller foundries in Walsall, is today still casting the brasses using the loose patterns method of over 100 years ago. The individual pewter patterns are pressed into the prepared box of foundry sand, usually ten at a time. The impressions are all joined by short cavities, usually at the hanger, to allow the molten brass to reach them when poured. There has also to be an outlet for the air, so a second cavity leads away from the bottom to ensure that the molten metal fills up the whole of the impression. The moulds are all stood on their sides to be filled. When filled, the moulds are opened and the brasses are removed, complete with the 'gets' attached top and bottom.

In the next operation the brasses are trimmed and the gets removed. At this point, present day manufacture begins to differ from that of 100 years ago. Today rough edges are only partially removed, but in the middle of the nineteenth century, the crude castings were worked on by hand, often in the cottage homes of the workers. The edges were hand-filed so that no flaws remained. Even the relief of the brass was touched up where the design did not show clearly.

In order to hold the brass securely in a vice without damaging the brass itself, two projections about three quarters of an inch long were cast into the back of the brass. After the touching up had been completed, the projections were cut off and usually filed smooth. It was a poor saddler who would hang a brass on leather with these projections not properly finished off, as any trace of them soon left tell-tale marks on the leather.

The final stage in the making of the brass was the polishing of the face. As sand castings have a rough finish the polishing was necessary to give it a smooth shiny surface. If the back of a cast brass is examined, the rough, sandy texture can be seen. Handmade brasses from sheet brass and the later stamped ones are as smooth on the back as they are on the face.

The stamping of the brasses from sheet brass seems to have started about 1880. The making of the metal dies to do this work was very expensive, and so were the machines, so that a manufacturer would have to be very sure of a good sale for the product before investing a lot of money. Only a few of the larger manufacturers could afford to invest in the necessary equipment to stamp out the brasses. The stamping of brass had first been carried out over a hundred years before being applied to the manufacture of horse brasses. However it would only be an economic operation if a large market were forthcoming and as this was the time of the peak use of horse brasses, stamping commenced.

At first the blank designs were cut out of heavy brass sheet and these were further cut out by operatives stamping one piece of the pattern at a time. Because of the irregularities in the resulting pattern, these are often mistaken for early handmade brasses. Later, thinner brass and heavier presses were used to stamp out the complete brass in one operation.

Our Country Inns have amassed better collections of harness and harness decorations than most of our museums. Here is a small part of the collection at the Croft Inn, Hythe, near Southampton, collected by the late Russel Gilmore. (*Russel Gilmore*)

When the demand for the horse brasses began to decline rapidly at the time of the First World War, it was the manufacturers of the stamped brasses who were the first to cease production. The manufacturers who carried on casting the brasses survived longer and today, all the brasses produced for the souvenir market are of the cast variety.

Brass was not the only metal used for making the face pieces. Others, including German silver (brass with a little nickel added), were used in small amounts and nickel in greater numbers. We have

Another fine pub
collection. Brasses
decorating the fireplace
of the Victoria Inn,
Llanbedr, near Harlech.
The studded breastplate
is typical of the N. Wales
area.
(*Ratcliffe Photographs*)

seen that the nickel brasses found most favour in Scotland and the coastal areas of England and Wales.

There was once a good export trade in brasses to countries like New Zealand, Australia and Canada. Special patterns were often produced for these countries. Even the small moon face brasses, once popular in Italy, were to be found in Matthew Harvey's catalogue at the end of the last century.

THE MANUFACTURER'S CATALOGUES

(Below and overleaf) Four pages of face piece patterns from the catalogue of Thomas Crosbie, c.1884. The pattern numbers were often cast into the back of the brasses. *(Ratcliffe Photographs)*

Many references have been made to the manufacturer's catalogues. For anyone interested in the harness trade, they are a mine of information. The first person to produce one was Thomas Newton whose great-grandfather had started the family firm in Walsall in 1735. His father induced the first of the successful saddlers' tool makers to leave Cricklade in Wiltshire and settle in Walsall. Thomas, born in 1810 started the ready-made brown harness trade in Walsall during the 1830s. At that time the only saddlers in the town were two black saddlers, or harness-makers.

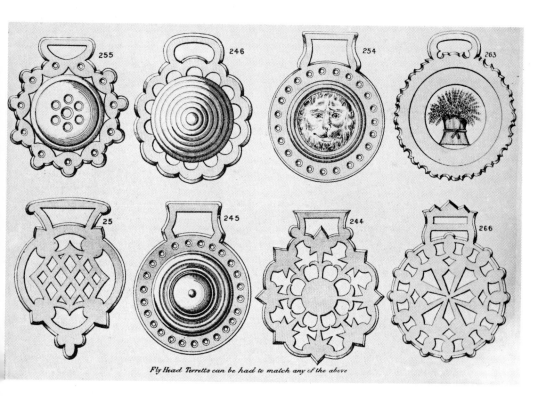

Fly Head Terrets can be had to match any of the above

Fly Head Terrets can be had to match any of the above.

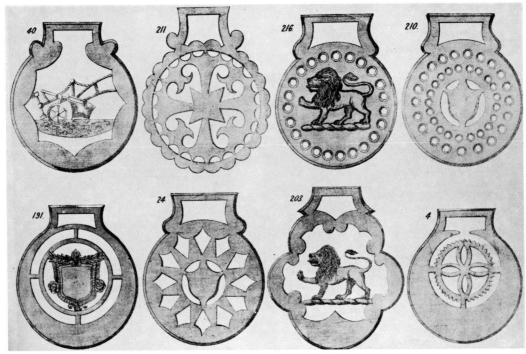

Newton had a gift for drawing and used it to produce a catalogue of drawing of the manufactures of Walsall. These he had lithographed and published under the title of *The Saddlery of All Nations*. The first edition appeared in the 1840s, and thirty years later a much improved version was published. This seems to have been the signal for other manufacturers to produce similar catalogues showing beautiful engravings of their range of products.

To the horse brass collector the study of these ctalogues can be very useful, especially as many of the manufacturers cast numbers into the back of the brasses which corresponded to the number of the pattern in the catalogue. Thomas Crosbie, of Birmingham, was one manufacturer who always cast the pattern number into the back of the brass, and occasionally into the front. The firm produced a *Pattern Book of Harness and Carriage Mountings*, c. 1885, showing hundreds of beautifully engraved pictures of their wares. William Overton, of Walsall, not only cast the pattern numbers on the brass, but most of their later designs had the initials W.O.W. also cast into the back. Their catalogue, produced in 1899 and revised c.1903 was a simple affair compared with earlier ones.

As an example of how useful a study of these catalogues, can be, one private collection included an old cast brass with the 'date'

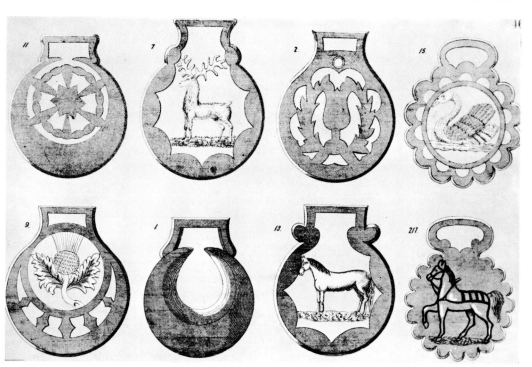

1849 engraved on the back. This later turned out to be the pattern number for that brass in the 1883 catalogue of the Walsall firm of Matthew Harvey, one of the earliest showing a list of designs of face pieces. They were described as being available in brass, nickel or German silver, cast or stamped.

Dozens of catalogues were produced by, not only the manufacturers, but the wholesale saddler's ironmongers as well. Probably the two best known were the *Equine Album* of Hampson and Scott, first produced in the 1890s, and the *Four in Hand* illustrated book of saddlery by the firm of R. E. Thacker. Their first edition was in 1895, followed in 1905 by the second edition. Both these firms' catalogues had hundreds of designs of the harness fittings and decorations and are well worth a study. They were originally sent out to prospective buyers, the saddlers and harness-makers, and are usually found with a saddler's name engraved on the cover.

HORSE BRASS DESIGNS

From the simple designs of the handmade brasses there developed very intricate patterns, the majority of which were based on a circle, a crescent or a star. The circle predominates because it is the simplest shape for a designer to start with. As a plain brass disc was not sufficiently decorative, patterns were added inside, either purely geometrical designs or more tangible objects such as the heraldic devices. Most of the simple designs inside a circle were regarded as representing the sun in some form or other by twentieth-century writers. Many of the circle designs were raised in the centre in the form of a cone, a shape used long before hanging brasses were manufactured, as rosettes, or temple bosses, fixed to the bridle at the junction of the brow-band and the head-strap. Porcelain was used in this shape of brass to make a more colourful design in the late nineteenth century. Red, white and blue were the popular colours.

(Opposite and overleaf) Two pages of face piece patterns from the Matthew Harvey catalogue *c.*1902. Matthew Harvey's were one of the largest firms to make brasses by stamping, and most of the above patterns were produced by this method. *(Ratcliffe Photographs)*

The crescent designs were also numerous. The plain crescent was produced by most manufacturers both in cast and stamped forms, and was easily the most popular of all horse brass designs. Complete breastplates of crescent brasses were common and a crescent was also very popular as a face brass-in most parts of the country. The crescent brass is probably one of the only patterns which can be continuously traced back in time as a decoration for horses. Some of the earliest decorations depicted on the ridden horse were crescents, and a high proportion of horse decorations unearthed from the past in both Britain and abroad, were of this shape. It could be that the crescent horse brass developed from a

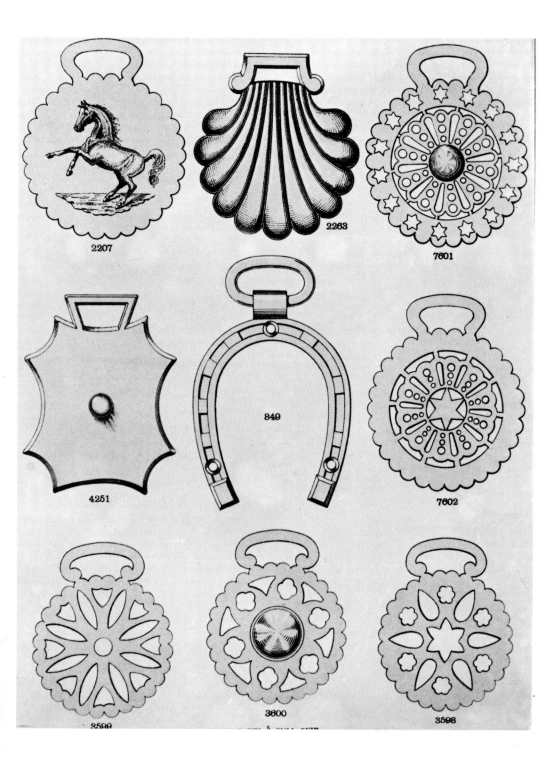

2207

2263

7601

4251

849

7602

3599

3600

3598

288

958

2565

362

5316

2323

horseshoe, but most likely it was one of the original handmade designs originating from southern Europe, where it was used in many forms.

The most common representation of the crescent is with the points upwards, but a number of manufacturers produced it with the points downwards. A triple design was also popular, particularly in Scotland, and a few brasses were produced with two crescents above a small patterned brass. The crescent was extensively used as a frame to enclose numerous other patterns and symbols.

Star shaped brasses were surprisingly uncommon though the star appears frequently inside other frames. They appear amongst the early handmade designs, but only kept their popularity locally, particularly in north Wales and the bordering counties where the five pointed pattern was most frequently seen. Stars with six, seven and eight points were also to be found.

The heart is a more common shape for a brass than the star. They were made both as plain heart brasses and also as a frame enclosing another pattern or symbol. The Staffordshire Knot is often found inside a heart and is particularly associated with Walsall. The Knot supporting a bear and ragged staff is the badge of the town of Walsall and this was produced in horse brass form.

Pure pattern brasses are very numerous and many of the designs are particularly beautiful. All sorts of interpretations have been put on the various designs by modern writers with varying degrees of credibility.

Easier to describe are the subject brasses, the motives of which were mainly lifted straight from the books of heraldry. These heraldic brasses were very popular amongst the carters and probably gave them the same feeling of importance as modern youth seems to get from wearing badges and representations of military ranks on their clothes. Some of the heraldic devices depicted include: the lion, horse and stag in various positions, the eagle, owl, martin, partridge, cockerel, phoenix, swan, dog, fox, ram, anchor and even the sailing ship.

Traders motifs were numerous. The early crossed saws design and the later tree and acorn designs could be worn on the horses of the timber traders. There were many early patterns of wheat-sheaf and windmill and later a sack, all of which could be used on the miller's horses. Brewers had a number of barrel designs to choose from, often having the company name inserted. One brewery company even produced a brass showing a representation of a bottle.

The carter could choose designs, associated with his trade; one brass showing a carter with his whip, another depicting the carter riding in his cart. A later design shows him appearing to be nodding off, but it is doubtful if it would have been popular amongst carters. The heavy horse in harness was depicted in a number of patterns. The design inside a frame shows typical Walsall pattern shaft harness, with double girth straps on the saddle. The later design, without a surround, shows a horse harnessed in trace gears. The horse's head inside a horseshoe frame is usually that of a riding horse though one manufacturer did produce a design where the head is wearing a blinkered bridle.

The horseshoe is naturally a common design for decorating the horse. It worries some folk that the designs invariably have the shoe 'with the luck running out'. The design is probably older than the superstition as the badge of the Worshipful Company of Farriers, granted in the seventeenth century, is three horseshoes, all with their points downwards.

For the ploughman there were old patterns of ploughs and a complete team of ploughman and his horses. For the farmer there were early designs depicting farm animals, including the ram, bull, cockerel, and of course the horse. The cow and sheep brasses appear to be quite modern designs.

The anchor and sailing ship patterns were said to be popular on the horses working for the dockyards, whilst the railway horses had numerous designs with early locomotives to choose from.

PRIVATE BRASSES

The railway companies led the field in producing their own designs with the company's monogram, ordered specifically for their own horses. Company monograms on the saddle and blinker brasses were common, but not so common were the actual horse brasses. Railway companies known to have produced their own designs include the Midland, Great Northern, Lancashire and Yorkshire, North Staffordshire, London and North Western, North Eastern and its successor the London and North Eastern. Another brass for the 'B. and L. Railway', probably the Blackpool and Lytham railway, in existence from 1863 to 1871, is known.

Many brewery companies also had private brasses with the company name inserted. They include Dale and Company of Cambridge; Oakhill Brewery Co., Georges Bristol Brewery; Butlers Brewery of Wolverhampton; and, still being worn today, Shipstones of Nottingham.

Many other private firms owned monogrammed brasses and particularly carriers like J. C. Wall and Thomas Bantock and Co., both of which were carriers for the Great Western Railway.

Local councils often ordered brasses for their own horses, either

Some private brasses; reading from *top to bottom*; an unidentified coat of arms; the crest of the William Butler Brewery, Wolverhampton; J. C. Wall carriers for the Great Western Railway; an R.S.P.C.A merit badge; North Staffs Railway Company; a saddler's brass from Hay-on-Wye; A private farmer's brass from Worcestershire. (*Ratcliffe Photos*)

J.C.WALL.

MERIT BADGE
R.S.P.C.A.
LONDON
CART HORSE
PARADE
1914

HARTWELL-MAKER-HAY

JGG

in the monogram form, as with Leeds and the City of London, or coats of arms, or badges, examples of which included Birmingham, Nottingham, Lincoln, Newcastle, Cardiff, Liverpool, Middlesex and, of course, Walsall.

Examples of farmer's brasses with the name of the farm and its location, are found, but as the brass decorations on a farm were usually the property of the wagoner and not the farmer, examples are rare.

Saddlers brasses are not so rare. They were produced as an advertising aid for the saddler and were most popular in the western half of England and Wales. Elsewhere the majority of saddlers used other ways of displaying their name on the harness. Occasionally a saddler would order a unique design for his own use, but on the whole, standard patterns were chosen and the names cast or chased into the design.

A saddler would hang a brass with his name on the top of a breastplate. There must have been well over 100 saddler's hanging brasses produced. In Penzance alone, there were named saddler's brasses for Richards, James, Ash, Lawrence, Millet and Nicholls and Son, the last named being the only saddler still working in the town.

COMMEMORATIVE BRASSES

The 1887 Golden Jubilee of Queen Victoria's reign, occurring as it did at the height of the horse brass era, seems to have started the fashion for the production of special brasses to commemorate an event or person. An earlier V.R. brass, dated 1870, could have been struck to commemorate Victoria's thirtieth wedding anniversary, but the reason for a similar design dated 1868 defeats the imagination.

Designs were often just adaptations of existing patterns, but many special brasses, with Victoria sternly depicted on them, were also struck. The head of Victoria was usually taken from the designs on the coinage. The young head seen on the 'bun' pennies, is the rarest, and usually appears on undated brasses. The diamond jubilee was also extensively celebrated in horse brass designs, as was Victoria's death, commemorated four years later. In all, over fifty commemorative designs of Victoria were produced.

The turn of the century also saw a design produced by William Overtons, of the National flags of Great Britain and France to commemorate the Entente Cordiale. A note in *Saddlery and Harness* of June 1900 gives an idea of the popularity of commemorate brasses.

'The patriotic horse ornaments introduced and registered by William Overton Ltd. have had an enormous sale, catching on as

A selection of royalty brasses from the author's collection. Royalty brasses did not appear in manufacturer's catalogues. Note the deterioration in design from that of Victoria to that of the present Queen.
(Ratcliffe Photographs)

they did just in time for the demonstrations celebrating the relief of Ladysmith and Mafeking.'

Although Edward VII had been depicted as the Prince of Wales, most brasses bearing his portrait appeared at the time of his coronation in 1902. Some of the designs were a rehash of the earlier Victoria patterns, but some entirely new ones were produced. One design describes the new King as 'The Peacemaker', but when George V was crowned there were very few peaceful years left before the Great War was to break out and herald the end of the horse brass era. In fact, the designs produced for the coronation of George V were probably the last serious attempt at designing horse brasses for use with the heavy horse harness. About twenty-five different designs were produced on this special occasion.

Because the occasions were so soon over, the commemorative brasses never found their way into the manufacturer's catalogues.

Later Royalty brasses were struck for Edward VIII (prematurely), George VI, and the present Queen on the occasion of their coronations, but few of the brasses have ever been worn on horse harness.

Other persons commemorated on horse brasses include Gladstone, Lord Randolph Churchill, Joseph Chamberlain, Disraeli, Lloyd George, and at the time of the Boer War, Baden-Powell, Lord Roberts and Kitchener. Nelson appeared at the time of the centenary celebrations in 1905 and at the end of the last war, designs of both Churchill and Montgomery arrived too late for many to have seen a horse.

Fred Archer enjoyed as great a popularity as a horse brass design as he did as a jockey, but how Abraham Lincoln managed to find his way on to a very English institution, is a bit of a mystery.

AWARD BRASSES

The first horse brasses struck as awards for showing horses in harness seem to be those R.S.P.C.A. merit badges of the London Cart Horse parade formed in 1886. It is probable that award brasses started being issued very soon afterwards. Certainly they were being issued in 1898 and carried on being issued, with the occasional modification, until the Cart Horse Society was amalgamated with the Van Horse Society, who had first issued award brasses in 1907. From 1896 the R.S.P.C.A. also issued a general award brass of circular design, intended for awards at other horse shows.

The period from 1900 to the outbreak of war in 1914 seems to have been the heyday for brasses awarded at local and National shows. Some of the local shows which produced award brasses in this period include: Lewisham and District Horse and Pony Show,

Sussex and Brighton horse parade, R.A.O.B. Worthing No. 1 Lodge, horse parade, Borough of Lambeth Cart horse parade, Bishops Stortford and district horse parade, Dunmow horse and cart parade, Acton horse parade, Winchester horse parade and Walsall horse parade. Many others also gave awards, but after the war finished only the London Cart horse parade and the Van horse parade continued to do so. The Ealing horse parade was revived after the Second World War and issued a special Victory horse parade brass and continued to award brasses till 1950.

(Below and overleaf). Fly head terret patterns from: *below*, Thomas Crosbie's, and, *overleaf*, Matthew Harvey's catalogues. This form of decoration first appeared in the middle of the 19th century. *(Ratcliffe Photographs)*

Also after the war, the old L.M.S. railway company awarded a special brass in 1947 at their own horse parade. A year later British Railways had taken over and brasses were awarded for at least another couple of years.

Winners at ploughing matches in the southern half of the country were often presented with brasses engraved with their names. These individual awards were so prized that they were kept by the

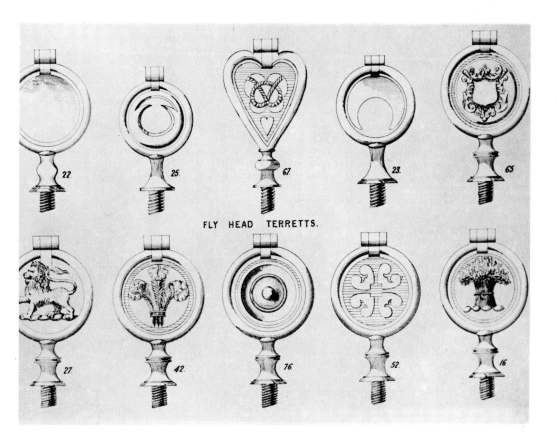

FLY HEAD TERRETTS.

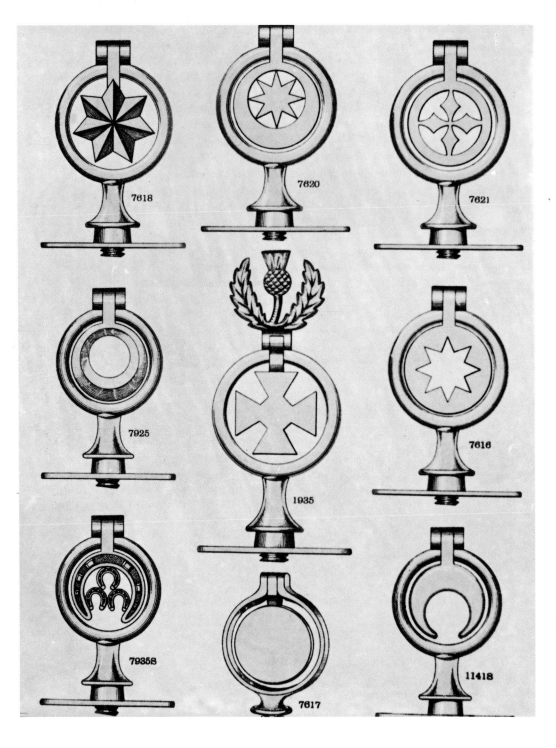

7618

7620

7621

7925

1935

7616

7935S

7617

11418

ploughmen and their families long after the rest of the brasses had disappeared.

OTHER BRASS ORNAMENTS

Fly head terrets were manufactured from about the middle of the nineteenth century. There were two methods of fixing them to the harness; by screw into a special fitting between the layers of leather as on the top of the head-strap, or the popular Scottish method of a long spike fitting into the stuffing at the top of the collar.

Their designs were almost as varied and numerous as those of the horse brasses, and many of the manufacturers' catalogues show fly terrets to match the face pieces. The majority took the form of a miniature version of a face piece fixed to swing freely inside a frame, usually circular. Even the royalty designs were made up as fly head terrets as well as other commemorative patterns.

The most frequently met pattern is a plain disc which is the best representation of the flashing sun disc said to ward off the evil eye. The carters' reasons for attaching them to the head-strap were chiefly for decoration, but to some they had a definite function, as suggested by the manufacturers' term, fly terret. Flies tend to make the horses restless in summer, by buzzing around their ears, and the movement of a fly terret helped, to a certain extent, to discourage the flies. In areas of Herefordshire, the fly terret is known as a leader, because the lead horse of a team usually wore one. The other horses wore ear-caps to keep off the flies, but the leader had to hear the carter's commands, and so wore a fly terret instead.

Some carters discarded the fly terrets in summer. Bert Colbourne of Eastbury describes why: 'When the flies were about, the horses didn't wear flappers (fly terrets) or brushes (plumes) because the horses nodding and shaking their heads would get them tangled up in each other's harness.'

The double fly terret, which had a double miniature brass pivoting on a centre pin, was particularly popular in Scotland, where it was usually known as a burler, or tumbler, because of its movement.

Even larger fly terrets were manufactured, more for the show harness and were usually attached to the saddle or the top of the crupper. Multiple terrets were popular in the south western counties and were often provided with fittings to take a plume of horsehair.

Plumes were usually coloured red, white and blue or combinations of these colours, and could be either stiff or flowing.

Before leaving the terrets, mention should be made of the so called 'pony brasses', the miniature editions of the horse brasses. Most of these brasses were produced for the souvenir trade using the patterns from the fly terret centres, and casting a hanger into the design. Pony brasses can be found made up from rosettes and the Sheffield stars (patterned brasses popular in that area and attached to the harness using wire studs). They usually have crudely attached hangers but were genuinely worn on the harness. A few early designs, such as the moon face one mentioned earlier, were produced and worn on pony or donkey harness.

Hame plates were specially produced by some manufacturers to decorate a strap between the tops of the hames, just above the point of the collar. Again, many designs were produced to match face pieces and fly terrets. The pattern with three walking horses on the top was particularly popular. Designs with both 'God Save the Queen' (Victoria) and 'God Save the King' (Edward VII) matched the royalty brasses. Firms often used the hameplate as the advertising spot for their company name.

In areas of Northumberland and Durham, and also in the south western counties, hameplates were a major decorative feature. The

(Below and opposite) Early hame plate patterns from the catalogue of Thomas Crosbie. Fewer hame plates were produced than face pieces and early examples are hard to find today. *(Ratcliffe Photographs)*

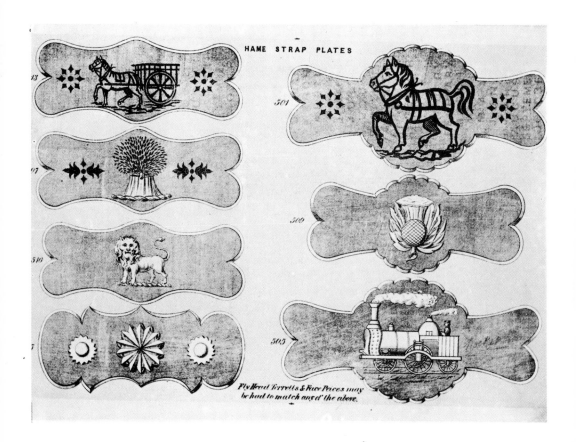

HAME STRAP PLATES

Fly Head Terrets & Face Pieces may be had to match any of the above.

northern version, known as a high level, was made in leather, with as many as ten pieces of brass decoration attached, sometimes including the saddler's name. The south western version was even larger and more decorative, usually incorporating a hameplate brass surrounded by other brass pieces.

Rosettes are one of the oldest form of harness decoration. The heavy horse borrowed them from the bridle of the racing horse and used them not only to decorate the point where the brow-band and head-strap meet, but also as decorations to slip over any straps on the harness, such as the loin and hip straps of the breechings.

The majority of rosettes were stamped with two or three dies being needed for the more protruding conical ones. Rosettes are still being made for the riding horse, but though the patterns still exist for the heavy horse harness, there is no market for them. Today it is only the souvenir trade which keeps the manufacturers of harness fixtures and fittings still producing any of the horse decorations.

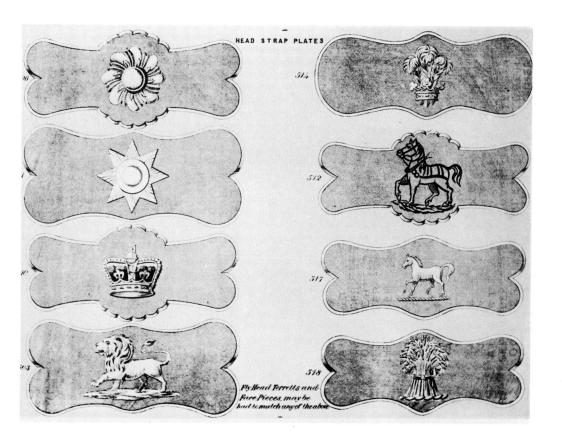

CHAPTER ELEVEN

Bells and Braiding

THE PURPOSE OF THE BELLS

Horses have worn bells for one reason or another since biblical times when 'Zachariah prophesied a day of peace when bells hung upon the necks of horses shall be inscribed "Holiness unto the land"'. However, the reason for the harnessed horse in Britain wearing bells was very much a functional one. The bells served as an advance warning to all that a team of horses was approaching, just as the modern car horn gives advance warning. The necessity for such a warning is apparent when one considers the state of our roads 200 years ago. C. Gray's commentary on Pyne's sketches in '*Microcosm*', 1849, includes the following description for the need to wear bells.

'Anciently the intercourse between different parts of the county was but trifling, as well as very irregular; and the goods were conveyed on the backs of horses, on that account called pack-horses.
This is the cause of the narrowness of such of our roads and bridges, as have not been widened since the general introduction of wagons, gentlemens' carriages, and stage coaches. Even still in these districts, where turnpikes have not been erected on the cross roads, we find many of them so narrow that two small carts cannot pass. On entering these, the driver is obliged to go forward and examine if any vehicle is coming, or else he halloos to give warning that he is advancing, and to make the carter, who is approaching, stop in the wide space at some gate which opens into the neighbouring fields. To this, perhaps, we may trace the origin of the use of bells in wagons and teams. Their sound put the parties, while yet at a distance, on their guard, not to advance too near where they could not pass, and could not well retreat.'

Team bells continued to be used for nearly another 100 years, though they finished up being worn more for their decoration than their utility as an advance warning system. Massingham, in *Country Relics*, tells of a Dorset farmer using the bells up to 1934. Albert Pain, of Peasmarsh, Sussex, remembers the last team of horses in the area with bells: 'A local farmer from Northiam had a team of horses which wore a full set of bells. You could hear them passing on their way to Rye. That would be the year the Lifeboat went down.' (In 1928 the Rye Harbour boat capsized on its way back from a mission with the loss of all hands.) There was a carter in west Oxfordshire still using bells in the 1930s for practical purposes.

It would be rash to suggest that narrow lanes and high hedges did not exist in the northern half of Britain, but it is a fact that the team bells worn by the horses were almost invariably found south of a line drawn from the Wash to Shrewsbury. The reason is probably that the use of bells was limited to wagon teams, and it is only in the southern half of the country that wagons were in general use. The need for wagon teams, in particular, to be furnished with the bells arises from the practical difficulty of backing a loaded wagon and its team, should they meet head on with another team in a narrow road.

Bells were also useful for warning other road users if the wagon had to finish its journey after darkness had fallen, as lights were seldom carried.

The use of bells by pack-horses was general over the whole of Britain. 'Till the middle of the eighteenth century, goods in Scotland were transported from place to place by pack-horses in gangs of thirty to forty. The roads being narrow, the leading horse carried a bell to warn those approaching from the opposite direction.' There are also pictures of pack-horses in trains and wearing hoops of open clapper type bells hung above their packs. The more usual pattern of bell depicted being worn by the pack-horse was the rumbler.

RUMBLER BELLS

The rumbler bells are hollow spheres of bell metal or iron which have been cast with a small ball of iron loose inside. They produce an unmusical rumble rather than the ring of the open clapper type. They were cast in one piece, complete with the iron ball, or rumbler,

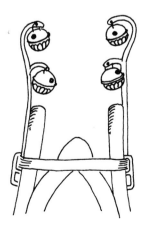

Fig 37 (left) Rumbler bell—with maker's name in traditional pattern markings

Fig 38 (right) Rumbler hame bells

inside. The process of manufacture has been described as 'a remarkable example of advanced pattern making emanating from the eighteenth century'. They were certainly made earlier than this. Salisbury Museum has various examples of 'late mediaeval rumbler bells'.

The makers followed a traditional pattern and even the designs cast into the surface of the bells took a traditional form. Most of the makers showed their mark within a circle at the bottom of the bell (Fig. 37).

There were a number of bell foundries in and around Wiltshire, including James Boroughs of Devizes and Cor of Aldbourne. But the most famed of all the bell founders was Robert Wells of Aldbourne. Not only did he produce church bells, but his foundry produced most of the team bells to be found in our museums and in private collections today. The initials R.W. are found on both rumbler and open clapper type bells. The firm was taken over in 1820 by the still extant Whitechapel foundry, and many of its original patterns survive to this day.

Rumbler bells by Robert Wells were made in sizes from 1 to 20. Each size has its own number cast into the bell, number 1 being the smallest and 20, a 6 in giant. The smallest were worn on straps round the pack-horse's necks, or as individual hame bells on iron mountings (Fig. 38). The largest are usually found fixed to frames in twos or threes and were mounted above the horse's collar from fixtures on the hames. The demand for these bells must have been quite substantial at one time, as the Whitechapel Foundry took over several duplicates of pattern equipment from the Robert Wells foundry.

TEAM BELLS

The rumbler bells could be tuned to different notes on the scale, but musically the open mouthed, clapper type of bell gave a better ring in the harmony produced when each set of bells rang its own chord. Most of the sets of team bells used were of the open mouthed type. Sets still survive for teams of four and even five horses.

Each horse in the team was furnished with a long rectangular frame, with a leather covering, which supported up to five bells designed to ring a chord. These were known in parts as a box of bells, or as a belfry. The bigger the bells were, the fewer were fitted to the frame and usually the horse nearest to the wagon wore the biggest.

It has been said that it was possible by listening to the bells of a team, to know to whom they belonged, because such was the genius of craftsmen like Robert Wells that they seldom had to produce two sets that had identical rings to them.

The leather housing which helped to protect the bells from the weather was often decorated with woollen fringing in the last century, but later brass fittings were more popular. The iron spikes either side of the box fitted into staples near the top of each of the wooden hames and to ensure that the bells hung perpendicularly they were usually set at an angle to compensate for the slope of the collar on the horse's neck.

In Herefordshire the method of mounting the bells and fixing them to the hames was different from the rest of the country. Here the bells were fixed on to large iron hoops, covered with leather and carrying as many as ten bells, each of a different size and note. Hereford museum has three sets of these hoops, with six, eight and ten bells mounted on them. There is also a pair of hames complete with the fittings which were needed to take the broader metal supports of the hoop. Because of the great weight of these hoops, the fittings were sited lower down the hames, and special straps were provided to steady them to the saddle. The overall width of the largest set at Hereford is 3 ft, and it stood 2 ft above the fittings on the hames. The weight of these bells must have been a serious hindrance to the unfortunate wagon horses wearing them—to say nothing of the deafening noise they must have produced just at the back of their ears.

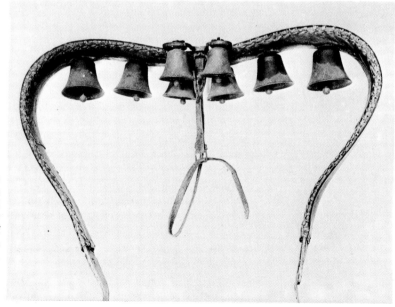

A set of team bells from Herefordshire; one of a set of three in Hereford Museum, all made by Robert Wells of Aldbourne. They were mounted on the hames using special fittings just above the tug hooks.
(*F. E. Morgan*)

The same museum also has a set of ten bells mounted in four tiers on an iron pyramid shaped frame. They are described as Ox bells and were possibly mounted on the wooden yoke of the oxen. More likely they were mounted on the front of the wagon to relieve the draught animals of the great burden they must have presented.

But the horses in the tale told by Horace Jones of Bridgnorth were each wearing their own set of bells that early morning when their wagoner set off for town. He had been up for most of the night polishing the harness and the brasses so that when he set off in the darkness he was still feeling sleepy, and the ringing of the bells and the jingling of the brasses hid the fact that there was no wagon trundling along behind. It was not till day-break that he discovered he had, in his excitement, forgotten to hitch the horses up to the wagon!

THE BRASS HARNESS BELLS

All the large team bells were cast by specialist bell founders, but the small brass harness bells which appeared in the middle of the nineteenth century were made with the rest of the harness furniture in centres such as Walsall. Our wagoner in the above tale would hardly have had the sound of his wagon drowned by the comparatively mild tinklings of these later bells. Even so, many carters would not subject their horses to the constant ringing of bells however small. Alf Edwards, who won many awards on May day, decorated the top of his horse's bridle with a single bell, but took the precaution of removing the clapper, for the comfort of his horse. 'Would you be able to hear what I'm saying, if you had a bell ringing a few inches from your ear all the time?' he pointedly asked.

But for showing off at ploughing matches and in the show ring, the wagoners went to town with the numbers of small brass bells they managed to fix on to the harness. Mr. Marden Green of Newbridge in Cornwall once showed a set of harness decorated with seventy-three bells, and recently David Trevenen of Penzance bought a horse specifically to start showing again harness and decorations with over 100 bells attached which his grandfather had once shown all over the south west.

A page of bell terret patterns from Matthew Harvey's catalogue, c.1902. There are firms in Walsall still making harness decorations to this day, though most find their way to the fancy goods and souvenir trades. (*Ratcliffe Photographs*)

Fly terrets with one, two or three small bells fitted were commonly used. Brass rosettes fitted with a hanging bell were fairly extensively seen on the straps of show harness in England and Wales. But the hanging horse brasses produced with one to three small bells fitted separately to the brass were relatively few and far between. Rarer still were the larger frames of bells produced mainly as saddle decorations. Elaborately designed frames supporting

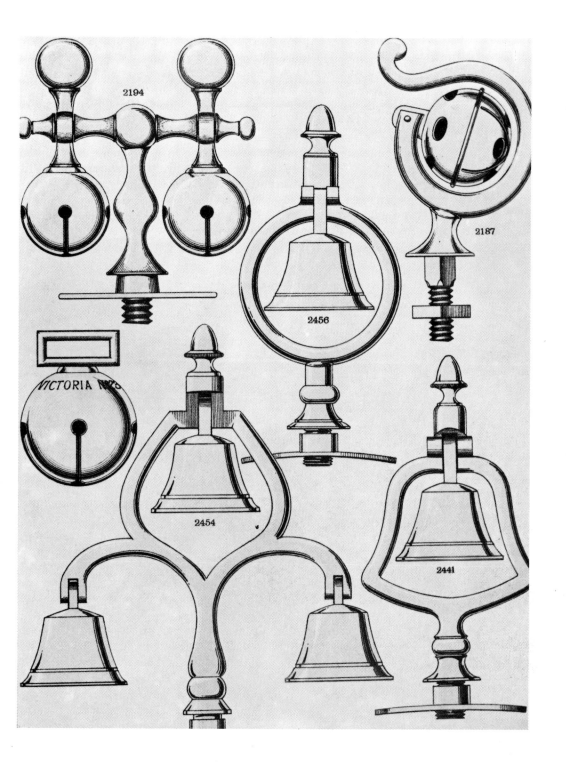

The most decorated set of harness ever produced! The late Fred Jelbert of Penzance with the display he showed all over the country. Designed by himself and made by Lanxon Bros. of Penzance, it was never beaten. Over 2,000 pieces of brass, including 320 bells, go to making up the decorations. The total weight of harness and decorations is $4\frac{1}{4}$ cwts. (*David Trevenen*)

as many as seven bells were made by Matthew Harveys of Walsall at the end of the last century. The wagoners were not slow in making up their own frames and fitting them up with enough bells to win a prize for the loudest peal at the show!

Slightly larger bells, known as chimes, were produced specially for mounting on the saddle. These bells were more of a dome shape and were provided with multiple clappers either inside or mounted on frames above so that they hung round the edge of the bell. One set of chimes, with three bells and multiple clappers, could produce the same sound effects as eighteen miniature brass bells, and if sound had mattered most at shows they should have been a must for every set of decorations. They had the sweetest music of all the bells worn. However, they were not produced in any large numbers and they appear in only two or three manufacturers' catalogues.

PLAITING MANES AND TAILS

This was a form of decoration definitely not found in a manufacturer's catalogue. The methods of plaiting the manes and tails varied not only from one part of the country to another, but also from one breed to another and at different times of the year.

Many horsemen plaited up manes and tails every day whatever the job to be done and whatever the weather. To them a horse was undressed if not braided up. Town horses were generally plaited up each morning, but on the farms the manes were seldom dressed, except for special occasions, like going into market. Tails, however, were usually plaited up every day during the winter to keep them out of the way of the reins and traces, and also clear of the muddy conditions prevailing. In summer the tails were usually partly plaited, but a length of hair was left to act as a swish to keep the flies at bay.

The reason for plaiting the manes was purely for show. Not only did it give the horse a neat appearance, but a skilful man who knew how to plait well could make a very ordinary horse look a first class one when he had finished. Watto Watson in the Lake District, having seen a horse he knew very well cleverly turned out at a local show commented, 'T'orse were nowt, but t' driver was an artist.'

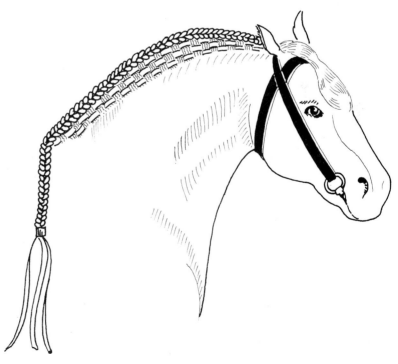

Fig 39
Full rig plait mane

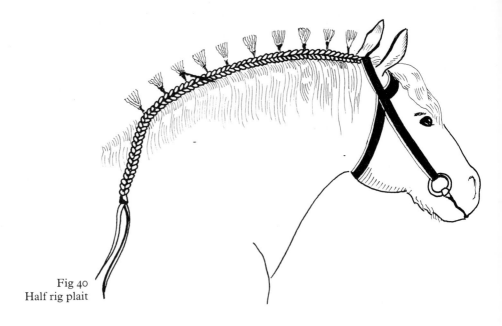

Fig 40
Half rig plait

A good man could show off the arch of the horse's neck by thickening the plait at the appropriate place.

The two commonest methods of plaiting the mane were: first to plait the whole of the mane on top of the neck leaving none of the hair hanging down (Fig. 39), and secondly to plait half of the hair in the mane along the crest and leave the other half to hang down the side of the neck (Fig. 40). The first method, usually called a full rig plait, was used mainly with the Suffolk and Percheron breeds, and the second method, the half rig plait, by the horsemen showing the Shires and Clydesdales. The full rig plait showed up the tremendous neck of the Suffolk and Percheron, but the other breeders generally saw it as an ugly form of plait.

To add more decoration and colour, bass, or raffia, and ribbon, or caddis, was braided into the mane. At one time wheat straw was used in the plait and the ears of the wheat were left neatly standing above the mane. Later flags, or standards, small pieces of ribbon fixed to lengths of wire about 4 in long, were worked into the top of the plait at 3 in intervals. Eight to ten flags were inserted in this way and their effect was to make the horse's neck look bigger.

One of the ways of giving a better appearance to a horse with a poor crest on the neck, a ewe necked one, was to insert a roll of cloth stuffed with straw between the initial parting of the mane before plaiting. As Mr. Fisher, of Holderness, explained, 'You had to make sure this was covered completely when plaiting as the use of a roll was frowned upon by the judges.'

Plaiting was started as near to the ears as possible and usually finished in a stream of ribbons or raffia. The colour of the ribbons used was usually chosen to suite the colour of the horse, though this varied from county to county. Greys in the north were decorated with red and yellow ribbons, further south in Yorkshire, green and yellow was used, in the Midlands red was considered to look best on a grey, whilst in parts of the Cotswolds, blue ribbon was favoured. Green and yellow were the colours extensively used for the Suffolk. In London, Ted Halliday described how the different contractors had their own ribbon colours, and the horsemen working for them chose the right colours so that other horsemen could tell which contractor they worked for.

The tails were braided in a number of different ways, the most popular of which were the Yorkshire bob, the Scotch bob, the half rig, the jug handle and the full braid.

The Yorkshire bob was probably the quickest and therefore the most used for daily work. All the hair of the tail was divided into three and plaited to the end of the dock. The ends of the hair were then split into two and brought back either side of the stump and twisted together again with some straw and tucked back into the plait. The addition of the straw was functional as well as decorative. Horsehair, like nylon, will not readily stay tied in a knot. By adding straw or ribbon to the plait, a knot can be tied which will not quickly come undone.

The Scotch bob started off similarly, but was made to look much tidier by working the plait more tightly. The bob was made smaller and enough plait left at the end to go round the bob, and again finish off with straw or ribbon.

Both these bobs were originally intended for horses with docked tails, to make their hindquarters look more prominent. Docking of horses' tails is now illegal and many horsemen still use the bob style of tail decoration, leaving the shorn stump of the tail to hang down below the bob in a very ugly fashion.

The half rig plait in the tail was used for summer shows, a length of loose hair left for the horse to keep the flies away. The outside hairs of the tail were brought together and plaited down the centre of the tail in a neat plait as thick as a horseman's thumb. To get the jug handle, or tail loop, ribbon or raffia was plaited into the hair and the plait carried on to the end of the tail. A piece of wire was often inserted in the end portion of the plait and a loop formed, the end being tucked back into the plait further up the tail.

176 THE HEAVY HORSE

Whatever the decoration used, whether a loop or the standards, they had to come up level with the top of the rump to give a good level appearance to the horse. The jug handle was a popular tail piece for the Shires.

The Suffolks and Percherons usually had their tails fully braided and the end doubled back and either tied there with two or three ribbons or often the whole tail was hidden with a binding of ribbon.

CHAPTER TWELVE

The Boat Horse

THE TYPE OF HORSE USED

The boat horse worked in a different world from the other draught horses. His world was that of the tow-path, and he was specially trained for that work. His master also lived in a different world from his neighbours and, like his horse, once brought into the world of the canals seldom ventured far away from it. His work, his tradition and his ways of living were all centred on the canals, and for this reason it is appropriate to treat his horse, the boat horse, separately from the other draught horses.

The boat horse was a special kind of horse, and yet it would be difficult to describe him. It would have been a rare sight to see an aristocrat of the heavy draught breeds, a pure Shire, Clydesdale or Suffolk in the harness of a boat horse. A boater was limited in height to 15·3 hands, no higher, because of the heights of the bridges along the tow-paths. He had to be able to pass under these bridges without discomfort. The tallest ones learnt to hold their heads to one side to avoid having their ears rubbed raw, especially when negotiating the few tunnels which were provided with tow-paths.

The boater had to be strong. A good boat horse could shift 50 tons on a good canal, one with a properly dredged channel and a well maintained tow-path. But it was not just strength alone. The horse had to be trained to move the load in easy stages. Once the boat was moving the job of keeping it going was much easier. It was estimated in 1810 that one horse and three men could move as much by barge as sixty horses and ten men could carry by wagon on the roads. The boater had also to be relied on to pull steadily for long hours. A horse could pull a loaded narrow boat at 2 m.p.h. and two together at 1½ m.p.h. Empty they could pull them at 3 m.p.h. and 2½ m.p.h. respectively. Said Alf Edwards, of Wolverhampton, 'The horses had to work hard and very long hours. We would keep them going as long as we could. The one horse would pull the boat all the way from Wolverhampton to Ellesmere Port. But in fourteen years of working this route we only ever had four different horses.'

The half-legged horse was the most popular type in use as a boater.

Canal companies supplied horses and harness to work their own boats, but there was also an independent boatman who owned his own boat and his horse and harness. He was known as a 'number one', and took an extra pride in his turn-out. Jack James was a number one and was brought up on the 'bread and lard' cut—the Oxford Canal. 'At certain places along the canal we could buy horses, usually from the didikaies. Often we would do a straight swop.' To a number one the horse came before the rest of the family, even when times were hard, simply because it was the horse that earned them their living. The horse, as head of the family, would be fed and bedded down at night before either the boatman or his family.

It paid the number ones to look after their horses, but not all boaters were so well treated. In 1836 the Mersey and Irwell committee heard that horses were 'often unmercifully flogged, and otherwise cruelly treated'. They appointed an inspector whose job it was to look out for any such offenders and to have them punished 'with the utmost severity of the law'.

Though there were a few horses 'just a bag of bones', the boater did not deserve the scorn so often poured on them by the rest of the horse world. One Oxfordshire wagoner recalled how 'anyone who had a horse which was a kicker or a bit fractious in any way would sell it to the canal companies'.

There was no love lost between the horsemen working on the land and those on the tow-paths. They lived in different worlds, but occasionally those worlds did meet and this often led to difficulties. A farmer from the Vale of Evesham illustrated one of the problems. 'We used to hire a lot of horses during the height of the growing season, for working between the rows of crops. One year we had a couple of the most awkward horses. No-one could work with them. They would walk with their front feet between one row and their backsides in another row. It was only when we sent them back that we learned that they had come off the canal.' A farmer hiring an ex-canal horse would also find great difficulty in making it go backwards. Canal horses had a built-in fear of backing into the water. Also they had never been taught to push back into breechings.

Mules and donkeys were also used for towing purposes. Mules were particularly liked because of their sure-footedness. The last long-distance, horse drawn boat in the Coventry area was drawn by a mule as late as 1954.

Donkeys were rather scornfully known as animals on the canals. Like the mules, they were very cheap to keep as they could live on next to nothing. A pair of donkeys took the place of one horse on some canals, especially those on the tributaries of the River Severn. Alf Edwards remembers, 'a fellow on the Stourport Canal who used to have a couple of donkeys pulling his boat laden with coal for Sharpness. They were coupled abreast and were faster than most horses. How they used to jostle each other when going under the arches! They towed to Stourport and then rode the barge on some straw which was thrown over the coal, whilst the current of the River Severn took it to Gloucester. They then towed the barge through the canal to Sharpness.'

WORKING THE HORSES

Horse towing paths were provided on all canals and on rivers above tidal points. They varied considerably from well kept and well surfaced ones to neglected tracks with overgrown hedges and in winter time more often deep in mud. Towing paths along riverbanks, were not fenced off from the neighbouring fields and where the fences and hedges came down to the water, gates had to be provided. One section of the Bedford Level was more like a steeplechase course. The horses were trained to jump stiles of 2 ft 7 in and, not surprisingly, they often gave themselves hard knocks.

Roving bridges carried the tow-paths from one side of the canal to the other. This was often necessitated by landowners refusing to have tow-paths on one side or the other. Some canals had these bridges built in two halves, leaving a slit in the middle wide enough for the tow rope to pass through. In this way the horse could carry on pulling as it crossed over the bridge and it was unnecessary to unhitch the barge. The barge would have to be cast off if, as on some older and cheaply built canals, no tow-path was provided under bridges. The horse would be uncoupled and led over to the other side of the obstructing arch to pick up its tow again. As few tunnels had tow-paths, whilst the barge was being 'legged' through, the horse was walked over the top to the exit, to be united with the barge when it re-emerged.

On some rivers where the tow-paths changed sides, no bridges were provided for the horses. They were taught to step on to the still moving barge and to step off again when the barge was brought close to the other bank.

Though some canal companies passed bye-laws ruling that a boy should lead the towing horse, and many of the early pictures show the horses being led or ridden, the horses were usually driven from behind. Said George Bodley, of the Midlands, 'We used a long rein of hemp or cotton and most of the time this would be fixed to the pegging noose as the horses were trained to work on their own.' To keep their horses moving, some boatmen tied a tin can to the rope behind the horse, or sometimes an old shoe or hollow-sounding clog, to make the horse believe that someone was in close attendance. Another dodge was to throw a stone into the water beside the horse, but if done too often, this could lead to the horse becoming shy of the water.

At locks, an experienced boat horse knew exactly when and where to stop and start, needing but few directions from the boatman who was thus free to give his whole attention to controlling the boat. Jack James worked with horses for many years. 'To start the horse we'd sometimes whistle or just say "Gee up, come on Charlie, buck up there," and to stop him we would just say "Wo Charlie". When turning the horse round, we always trained him to face the water so that he would never fall into the cut. The horse was always very cautious about backing and we would take him by the bridle and collar and gently coax him back with "Back Charlie, come on back Charlie."' To stop a boat the horse would be 'drawn in' and the nose of the boat turned into the mud by the bank.

A race would often develop to reach the lock before a boat coming in the opposite direction. Arguments quickly started as to who was there first and arguments often turned to fists being used. Said Jack James, 'If you couldn't fight, you weren't a boatman, and the women was as good as the men.' The Manchester, Bolton and Bury Canal Company set a fine of ten shillings for 'all cases of furious driving on the canal banks', in an effort to stop the races for the locks.

Where a canal had a steady traffic of full barges in one direction and empty in the other, for example, taking coal from a pit head, the horse pulling the empty barge had to stop on the inside of the tow-path when a loaded barge came by in the opposite direction. The straining horse of the laden boat could thus step over the towing line of the empty boat without losing any of its momentum.

THE HARNESS

The towing line ran from the horse's harness to a 4 ft high mast about a quarter the length of the boat from the bow. This was high enough to keep the line off the tow-path but not too high to catch the bridges.

The harness, known as boat gears in the Midlands and as tackle elsewhere, is typical leader or trace harness as described in Chapter Six. At one time chain traces were used, but in later years rope traces covered with wooden spoles, or bobbins, came into general use. The bobbins, each about 4 in long and resembling large wooden beads, prevented the ropes chafing the horses. In some areas leather tubes covered the ropes in place of the bobbins.

The traces were attached to a swingle tree or a spreader bar. The spreader bar would have a short chain at either end, meeting at the pegging noose, to which the towing line was attached. Swingle trees had a swivel hook at the back to take the tow line.

The bridle was blinkered and usually of the pattern local to the area where it was made. Although many 'shut up' collars were worn, it was more usual to find open collars 'with a big brass buckle on top'. Some horses would only work in a breast collar, and these were used successfully. The hames, to avoid them catching on the arches of the bridges, were cut down as low as possible. For the same reason, if a housen were worn, it would be a very small one.

Some saddlers, working close to the canals, specialised in catering for the needs of the boat horses. Jack James remembers how 'Mr. Dunn of Banbury would come down to the lock side and measure your horse up for a set of new harness whilst the lock was filling. We would also go down to his shop for old collar flocking which we used for making our mops.'

A number of canal companies enacted that horses be 'muzzled unless they are grazing'. This could have been to prevent them biting each other when passing, but more probably it was to prevent them pulling at the hedges as they walked along.

A very essential item of the horse's gear was its nose tin, from which it was fed. Again Jack James recalled how 'there were certain bridges on the route where the horse knew a tin of corn was due, and he'd stop there till the corn was given him. He would then walk along at an easy pace, eating out of the tin as he went. We would occasionally have to go forward and tighten the nose tin strap so

A horse-drawn barge on the Oxford Canal in 1936. The horse is having a feed from its nose tin. The bobbins on the traces are to keep the horse's sides from being rubbed. (*Radio Times Hulton*)

that the horse could get at the remaining corn. We usually eased up too and had a cup of tea whilst the horse had his nose tin. The women always kept tit-bits, usually lumps of sugar, in their apron pockets. These were fed to the horses at the lock side. Baskets were used instead of tins on some canals.'

THE DECORATIONS

The nose tin was decorated in the traditional painted designs of the canal people, who liked to use bold colours. The strong colours were also used for painting parts of the harness—a style of decoration peculiar to the canal boatmen. The bobbins were painted in different colours so that the traces resembled giant necklaces of coloured beads. The spreader bar was also painted in strips of contrasting colours, and often the hames were similarly 'painted like a barber's pole'. This practice of painting the parts of the harness was a relatively recent development. It seems to have started about the beginning of this century.

Red, white and blue were the May-day colours, and on most of the canals May-day was an important day for the boatmen and their families. They were gay folk by nature, but for the 1st May they set out to surpass themselves. They would often be up the whole night preparing not only the horse and the harness, but also the boats and themselves, 'for the women always poshed up on May-day'. There was keen competition amongst the boatmen to be more 'swanky' than the others. Said Jack James, 'The number ones always had the best turn-outs, and on some of the swankiest sets of harness you couldn't see the horses for brass.' Whilst the men groomed the horses the women and children polished the brasses.

At one time the horses were brassed up every day, but in later years the brasses were stowed away on board, especially during the winter months when the tow-paths had deteriorated into muddy tracks. On May-day the brasses were brought out again and face pieces and breastplates glittered in the sun, together with side pieces attached to the back strap and worn 'down the line'. Swingers were sometimes worn and occasionally the brass bells. There was also a fashion for threading brass rosettes on to the hip straps as well as the bridle. The rosettes would often be fitted with brass bells or ribbons.

Ribbons were tied, not only on to the horse and its harness, but to the boat also. Each canal had its own colours of ribbons. The canal Jack James was brought up on had dark blue as its traditional colour. 'These ribbons would be worn also on the day of the Oxford and Cambridge Boat Race. We were known as the Oxford Jews.'

Pieces of coloured wool were often plaited and tied to the buckles of the harness.

Bearing reins were decorated with the small brass hearts, diamonds, crescent etc. Hearts and diamonds were common patterns seen amongst the canal brasses as they also were on the harness of the gipsies' horses. Canal folk were often looked upon as gipsies because of the similarity of the life they led and of their traditions, especially in the style of their painting and decorations. In fact, as any canal folk were quick to point out, gipsies in Monkey boats were as rare a sight as were boatmen driving through the leafy lanes in barrel top wagons.

Though May-day was probably the brightest day in the boatman's year for making his turn-out 'swanky', in fact they decorated their horses and boats as often as they could find excuses. Weddings, births, christenings or any other special days were made good reasons for showing off the boats and the horses.

Many local shows near to the canals had special classes for the boat horses. Alf Edwards showed horses in this class at West Bromwich Show in the 1920s. He would probably have worn the traditional spiders web belt of the boatmen, traditionally renewed every May day. The small brass fittings for the harness were purchased from the saddler to decorate these belts. His horse would have been wearing the traditional ear-caps so loved by the boatmen. According to George Bodley, 'They were usually crocheted in different colours—you could choose your own. Mrs. Chatwin, who lived beside the bottom lock at Marsworth, near Tring, used to make them for the canal people. You ordered them on the way through and picked them up on the way back.'

FLY BOATS AND ICE BREAKERS

A form of high-speed travel was introduced on some canals especially the Grand Union and the Shropshire Union canals in an attempt to compete with the railways. In specially designed boats, express passenger and freight services worked day and night at speeds of 10 to 12 m.p.h. The horses were worked in teams of from three to eight, sometimes coupled in pairs and changing at intervals of five to ten miles. Their pace was a fast trot and after five miles of this the horses would be rapidly tiring. The work was hard and at the end of a long run the horses' shoulders would be rubbed raw on one side because of the difference between the direction of travel and the angle of pull to the boat.

When the railways were developed the canals lost most of their passenger services, but freight continued to be moved in express fly boats. The boats were light and shallow 'about a four plank boat only drawing 18 in and designed to carry 17 to 18 tons'. Once speed had been achieved the bow tended to lift out of the water to give a planing effect.

Fly boats had priority over all other canal users. If any boater should be foolish enough not to get out of the way quickly, his rope would be cut so that it did not interfere with that of the fly boat. At locks too they had priority, and no matter how much nearer other boats were to the lock, once a fly boat came in sight everyone had to give way to let it through the lock first. Four men worked them day and night, two on and two off duty at any one time. On the Grand Union, outriders usually rode the first horse, but on the Shropshire system they were driven from behind. The last of the fly boats ran on the Shropshire Union till just after the First World War.

In contrast to the speed of the fly boats, one of the slowest forms of transport on the canals, and one which occasioned great jollifications for the boatmen, was the ice-breaker (below). Once thick ice had formed on the canals they came to a standstill. The canal

Working the ice breaker on the canals was always a time of great merriment. Here, fourteen horses are ready to tow the ice breaker whilst a large party stand on the boat ready to rock it to and fro. (*British Waterways Board*)

company would then organise an ice-breaker to cut a way through for the boats. In the old days as many as twenty horses with their keepers were hired to tow the ice-breaker, and many more men were employed to stand on the boat and rock it about. 'Baiting money' was supplied for the horses by the canal company and free beer for the men. The more free beer the men consumed the better they were able to rock the boat and the less likely it was to ride up on the ice. Ice breaking was great fun and everyone had a good time.

Horses worked on the canals in considerable numbers well into the present century, but with the rapid decline of canal transport since the last war they have virtually died out. The few that remain have been recruited to tow pleasure boats.

Many of the boats used to carry a horse's tail on the tiller because the boatmen became so attached to their horses that when they reached the end of their useful life the tail was cut off and hung on the tiller as a memento. 'Most of them were cow's tails', argued Alf Edwards! But then the canal boatmen were always a breed of their own and they loved an argument.

Conclusion

There has in recent years been a revival of interest in the heavy horse. Is there a place for the heavy horse in our modern society now and in the future?

A small East Anglian brewery recently returned to using horses and drays for local delivery after an absence of twenty years. The reason was one of economics plus an enthusiasm for the heavy horse. The initial cost of a horse and dray is about 50 per cent less than the equivalent cost of a motor vehicle of similar capacity. What is more, the working life of a heavy horse and its dray is longer than that of a lorry, so depreciation costs are lower. So too are the day to day running costs, including shoeing, veterinary bills and food. The highest costs encountered in running lorries arise from the cost of the road fund licence and the tax on fuel, neither of which have to be met by horse-drawn transport.

Of course the lorry scores hands down on the question of speed, especially over long distances, but where town delivery work is involved, within a few miles radius of the loading point, the horse-drawn vehicles is more economical. The more the lorries are slowed down by traffic congestion and the higher the taxes imposed on road vehicles and their fuel, the more economic the horses will become.

To add to this, most users of the heavy horse for delivery work today take full advantage of the excellent advertising value which the horses present. Horse and drays on the streets are rare enough to be eye-catchers and thus good media for advertising.

All these figures have been proved and yet the heavy horses are still a rare sight. What is lacking most amongst those firms which could make use of horse-drawn transport is the enthusiasm and confidence in the horse's future to re-build stables and produce a modern fleet of horse-drawn vehicles. Twenty to thirty years ago there was a definite move to rid the streets of all horse-drawn transport in an effort to speed up the flow of through traffic in cities. Modern thinking on city planning with its traffic free areas is less opposed to the idea of a slower form of transport for delivery outside the main traffic flows and this should be to the horse's advantage. This could lead to a serious revival in the use of the heavy horse as a means of delivering goods.

On the farm there has also been a mild interest shown in bringing back horses for certain types of work. The constant use of heavy tractors, especially on heavy land is producing a hard pan below the level of soil cultivated—resulting in poor yields. It is argued that the use of horses for cultivation work would eliminate this problem. However, it is more likely that the equipment manufacturers will solve the problem long before it becomes necessary to return to horses. The horse can be used advantageously for odd jobs about the farm, and also put to work on wet heavy land where a tractor would cause problems, but the economic advantages are less easily proved than for the town delivery horse. Small holders, in particular, find horses an economic proposition and more than one who has given up tractors has been able to point to increased yields. But again lack of enthusiasm and feeling for horses are the main factors holding back their return to the land. However, the position is very slowly changing in the horse's favour.

General enthusiasm for the heavy horse can be built-up by those societies dedicated to keeping the heavy horse to the fore, and the best way they can do this is to take greater advantage of the spectacular qualities of the heavy horses. The return of the heavy horse classes to our shows should have greater encouragement, especially those classes which provide a spectacle for the public—the decorated harness classes, and others like the competitive driving classes that

The Breweries have for long been the main supporters of the heavy horse used commercially in Britain. They have shown that horses can be more economical than lorries over short hauls. Here are a pair from Whitbread's fine stable, used for delivery work in the City of London. (*Whitbread & Co.*)

The most up-to-date
horse drawn vehicle in
Britain. Vaux brewery
of Sunderland use this
tanker to serve the most
modern cellars near to
the brewery.
(*Vaux brewery*)

The recently formed
Southern Counties
Horse Ploughing
Association's champion-
ships at Alton attracted
eighteen teams of
decorated horses in
October, 1971. Events
like these, providing a
fine spectacle for the
public, hold one of the
keys to the survival of
the heavy horse in
Britain.
(*Photo: Author*)

were once a feature of shows in the east of England. Above all the re-introduction of drawing matches—where teams of horses compete against each other at pulling weights, would go a long way towards popularising the heavy horses. Drawing matches are very popular in America and they have been responsible for much of the present enthusiasm for the heavy horse breeds in that country.

The re-introduction of horses-only ploughing matches such as those organised by the Southern Counties Ploughing Association, are drawing more and more competitors and spectators—not because of the quality of the horse ploughing compared to that of tractor ploughing, but because the event is such a spectacular occasion, and surely this is the direction in which the efforts of the various heavy horse societies must be drawn. It is the vast new leisure industry which has preserved for all time the steam locomotive and traction engine and once more turned them into economic propositions. It can do the same for the heavy horse.

Our present day agricultural shows could well look back to the splendour of the heavy horse turnouts in the past, and do everything possible to encourage their re-appearance. Fine turnouts like this one from the past could well be a feature of all our future shows. (M.E.R.L)

Glossary

Because of the multiplicity of names applied to the various parts of the heavy horse harness in different areas of the country, a list of most of the terms met with during talks with horsemen is set out below. As well as the horsemen, the saddlers and manufacturers also had their different names for the same parts of the harness. This often led to confusion when saddlers were writing about their trade. In *Saddlery and Harness*, March 1904, an appeal was made through the Improver's Columns for a list to be compiled of all the variations in the names of the harness parts. Unfortunately only a few replies were published, not enough to give a comprehensive list.

There is still much work to be done collecting these local names, but the lists below should give the reader an idea of the widely differing terms to be met with when discussing the heavy horse harness.

The words in **bold** are those used in the text.

GENERAL HARNESS

harness	general term used from Cornwall to the north of Scotland.
GEARING	Yorkshire.
GEARS	widespread use in England and Wales.
GRAITH, GREATH	a Scottish term for harness, especially in S.W. Scotland.
HARNISH	local variation; Midlands, southern Scotland.
TACK	usually applied to riding harness, but also used to describe heavy horse harness in the west of England and Wales.
TACKLE	Midlands and S.W. England.
plough harness, gears etc.	widespread and common over Britain.
BACKBAND	Yorkshire.
BACKBAND AND THEATS	N.E. Scotland.
BACKROPES	S.W. Scotland.

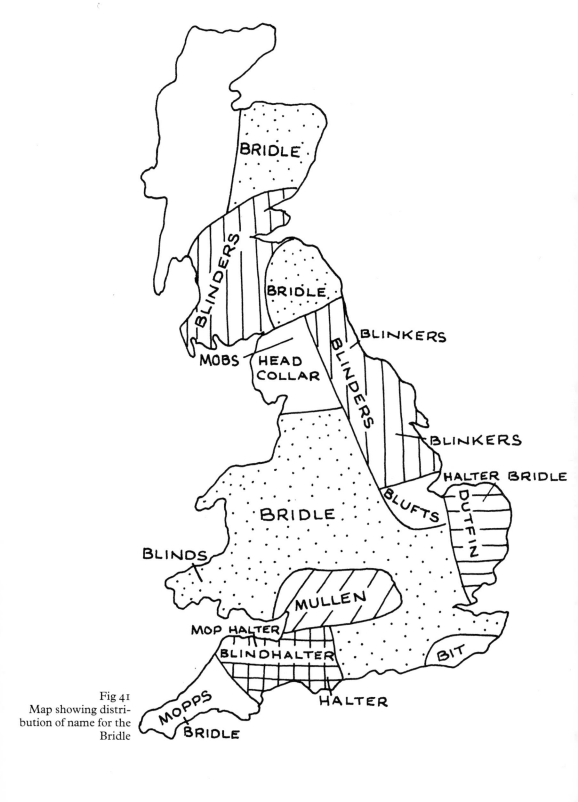

BRIDLE

BLINDERS

BRIDLE

BLINKERS

MOBS

HEAD
COLLAR

BLINDERS

BLINKERS

HALTER BRIDLE

BLUFTS

DUTFIN

BRIDLE

BLINDS

MULLEN

MOP HALTER

BLINDHALTER

BIT

MOPPS

BRIDLE

HALTER

Fig 41
Map showing distri-
bution of name for the
Bridle

BODKIN AND CHAINS	Lincolnshire.
CRUPPER AND CHAINS	Hertfordshire.
GEE OH, G.O., JOE	south Midlands to Welsh borders (derived from the command to come around to the right—gee oh—repeated constantly when ploughing).
PLOUGH CHAINS	widespread.
PLOUGH TRACES	widespread use in England and Wales.
PLOUGH TRAITS	Lincolnshire.

The name given to the horse yoked in shafts, trace or plough harness was usually applied to the harness as well. Thus the 'shaft horse' wore 'shaft harness' or 'shaft gears'.

shaft harness, gears etc.	in widespread use—particularly by the harness trade.
BRITCHEN	S.W. counties (because only the shaft horse wore breechings, this item of harness often gave the local name for the complete shaft harness).
CART	common over Britain.
FILLER	eastern England.
HIND	Sussex.
PHILL	S.E. England.
QUILLER, QUOILER, COILER	Kent, Sussex.
SHAFTER	Shropshire.
THILL, THILLER	southern half of England (an Old English word for thill＝shafts).
WHEELER	often used for town pole harness. An army term.
trace harness, gears etc.	the most commonly heard term for this harness.
CHAIN	widespread but not as common as trace.
CRIPPENS	S.W. England.
FORE	south Wales and S.W. England.
FORREST, FOREST, FOOREST	eastern England.
FOST HOSS	Yorkshire.
	north Wales.
LEADER	widespread use especially by the trade.
LEADING	Lancashire.
LONG GEARS	Midlands.

Fig 42
Map showing distri-
bution of names for the
hames

HAMES

HEMS

YEMS
HAME STICKS

HAMS · YAMS

HAMES

HOMES

HAMES

HAMES

SEALS · SAILS

TEES

COLLAR TREES

TUGS

HAMEWOODS

COLLAR TREES

HAMZES

COLLAR STICKS

THEAT	southern Scotland (from theat = chains).
TRACEN	N.E. Scotland.

HARNESSING TERMS

Other names given to the horse according to its position in a team:

BODY	E. Anglia and southern England (the horse next to the shaft horse).
FOOTER	west Midlands (the horse nearest the plough when ploughing in line).
FURROW HORSE	general use (offside horse walking in the furrow when ploughing abreast).
HANG BY HORSE	Yorkshire (nearside horse when ploughing abreast).
LAND HORSE	general use (nearside horse when ploughing abreast).
LINE HORSE	Yorkshire (the horse wearing the lines—reins—usually the middle horse if three abreast).
MIDDLE HORSE	general use (the middle horse in a team if working in line or abreast).
PIN HORSE	widespread (next to the shaft horse).
ROD HORSE	Kent (the horse in the shafts).
SECOND FORREST	eastern England (the horse next to the leader).
SECOND FOSS HOSS	Yorkshire (the horse next to the leader).
abreast	horses were worked 'abreast' over the whole of Britain.
bodkin	Yorkshire, Lincolnshire (two horses in line in the furrow and one land horse).
in line	a common term over most of England.
AT LENGTH	Midlands.
SINGLE	southern Midlands.
a-TRIP	southern England.
unicorn	general use (one horse yoked in front of and between a pair).

Fig 43
Map showing the
distribution of names for
the fly head terret

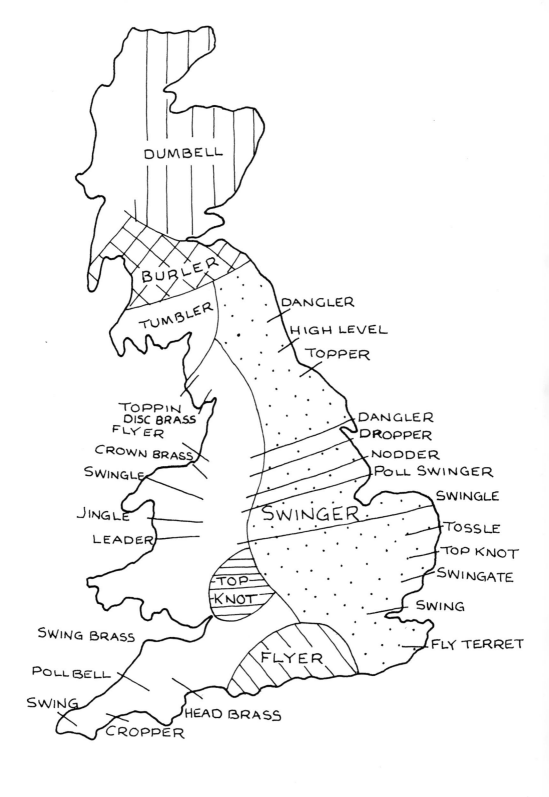

DUMBELL

BURLER

TUMBLER

DANGLER

HIGH LEVEL

TOPPER

TOPPIN
DISC BRASS
FLYER

CROWN BRASS

SWINGLE

JINGLE

LEADER

DANGLER

DROPPER

NODDER

POLL SWINGER

SWINGER

SWINGLE

TOSSLE

TOP KNOT

SWINGATE

SWING

FLY TERRET

TOP
KNOT

SWING BRASS

POLL BELL

SWING

FLYER

HEAD BRASS

CROPPER

THE PARTS OF THE HARNESS

The names for the chain which went over the saddle to hold up the shafts have a definite pattern to them:

back chain	common to the southern half of England.
BACK BAND	common to the northern half of England.
BACK STEEL	Yorkshire.
RIDGE CHAIN	Surrey.
RIDGE UP	Huntingdonshire.
RIDGER, REDGER	Kent.
RIDGEWORTH	Lancashire.
RIGET, RIDGET	Hertfordshire, Cambridgeshire, Northamptonshire.
RIGBODY, RIGBURY	Fife.
RIGWIDDY	mid Scotland (rig=ridge; withy= a rope, especially one of osiers).
RIGWOODIE	N.E. Scotland.
RISTIE	Hampshire.
RUDGET, RUDGE CHAINS	Cotswolds.

Even a very localised piece of harness can have a host of names. Where an iron bar was used over the saddle instead of a chain, especially in south east England and the west Midlands, where they were used when ploughing in line, some of the names used for the piece of iron were:

BAIL RIDGER	Kent.
BAR	Shropshire.
BEND	Herefordshire, Shropshire.
CRANK	Shropshire.
FOOTING IRON	Shropshire.
REDGER BAR	Kent.
blinkers	in general use over Britain.
BLINDS	common, especially N.E. England and Scotland.
BLUFFS	Yorkshire.
WINKERS	Ireland, and term generally used by trade.
breechings	in general use, though used more by the trade.
BACKBONE BREECH	west Wales.
BACKETY	Somerset.

Fig 44
Map showing the distribution of names applied to the men who worked the horses

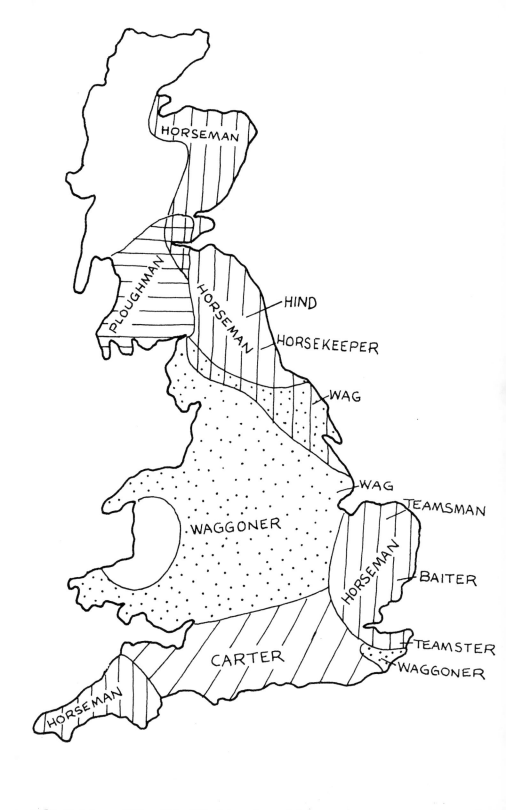

BRITCHEN	most commonly used term from Cornwall to Aberdeen.
CRIPPENS	Surrey.
QUILLER, QUOILER, COILER	Kent, Sussex.
STAYS	N.W. England.

bridle   see map fig. 41.

collar	in common use over the country.
BARFIN	Yorkshire.
BARPHAM	Cumberland.
BRAFFIN	Durham and Lake District.
BRECHAM	Scotland.
BRIME	Northumberland.
NECK COLLAR	N.W. England (in those areas where a bridle is known as a 'head collar').

The Scottish peaked collar was known outside Scotland simply as a 'Scotch collar', but inside Scotland it had its own variety of names.

LONG TOP	S.W. Scotland.

peaked collar or **brecham**   in general use over Scotland.

TOPPED, HIGH TOPPED	eastern Scotland.

The non-peaked collar was distinguished from the peaked one by a number of terms:

COWIE	Fifeshire.
DODDY	N.E. Scotland (after the Aberdeen Angus cattle—meaning hornless).
HUMMEL	N.E. Scotland (hummel=horneless).
LOW	general.
SHORT TOP	S.W. Scotland.

In the south-west of England, where open collars were the rule, the ordinary closed collar was a 'shut up' collar or a 'closed top'.

BUCKLE COLLAR	Dorset, Hampshire.
LATCH COLLAR	Cornwall.

open collar   general and trade name.

SPLIT COLLAR	general.

The names given to the collar designed to fit a horse with a prominent windpipe were:

pipe collar   general and trade name.

THROTTLE COLLAR	Dorset.
WINDPIPE COLLAR	mid-Scotland.

Fig 45
Map showing the distribution of the various commands for turning horses to the left
R—indicates those areas where reins were primarily used and no distinct voice commands were known

hames   see map fig. 42.

housen	general over most of England and used by the trade.
BRAFFIN TOP	Durham.
CAP	eastern England.
CAPE	old name, in general use in southern England.
COLLAR TOP	N.W. England.
FAN	Norfolk.
HAME BONNET	N.E. Scotland.
HAWSEN	Dorset.
HIGH LEVEL	Durham.
HIGH TOP	Yorkshire.
HOOD	Wales, Devonshire.
HOOSEN	Shropshire.
HOUDEN	Dorset.
HOUNCE	eastern England.
HOUSING	widespread.
HUSSIN	Worcestershire.
KNUB	Cambridgeshire.
OUNTS	Warwickshire.
SCOTCH TOP	Yorkshire.
TOP FLAP	Somerset.
TOPPIN	north England.
WEATHER PAD	southern Scotland.
saddle	common to most of Britain.
PAD	usually refers to lighter driving harness and pole harness but also used to describe the cart saddle in south of England.
PANEL	Cornwall.
STRADDLE	Ireland.

That piece of harness fixed between the trace chains to keep them apart and away from the horse's flanks had its local following:

spreader	in general use over most of England and Wales.
SPREAD BAT	Sussex.
STENT	west Wales.
STRETCH STICK	Kent, Sussex.
STRETCHER IRON	Yorkshire.
STRITCHER, STRETCHER	Yorkshire, Durham.
THEAT BAR	Fifeshire.

Fig 46
Map showing the distribution of the various commands for turning the horses to the right

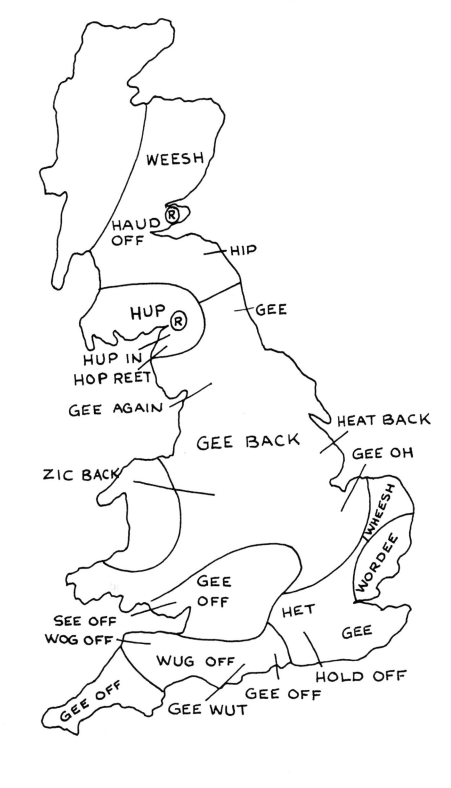

There is some confusion about the naming of the swingle tree and its parts. Some areas refer to a two-horse set of swingle trees, or a three-horse set. In other areas the swingle trees were only that part of the set immediately behind the horse, the other parts having names of their own. Where known, these names have been included— e.g. swingle tree and maister tree: Fifeshire.

swingle tree	general over Britain.
BADEKINS	Devonshire.
BATTEKINS	Herefordshire.
BODKINS	Berkshire.
BODKINS AND WAVE BEAMS	Somerset.
COBBLE, CIBBLE TREES	Yorkshire.
DRAUGHT BARS	south England.
HEEL TREES AND BAULK	Lincolnshire.
LAND TREES	Worcestershire.
SWING TREES	Suffolk.
SWINGLE TREE AND MAISTER TREE	Fifeshire.
SWINGLE TREE AND THRIB TREE	N.W. England.
SWIVELS	Oxfordshire.
TAWTREES	Shropshire.
TRIPLE TREES	Cambridgeshire.
WHIPPENS, WHIPPINS	south England.
WHIPPIN TREE	Pembrokeshire, Devonshire.
WHIPPINS AND BOLTS	Oxfordshire.
WHIPPLE TREES	S.E. England.

THE DECORATION

There were many regional terms for decorating the horses before going into town etc.

TO BRASS THE HORSE UP	a general term heard in many areas.
TO PUT ON ONE'S FAN	Norfolk.
TO PUT ON ONE'S FLASH	mid Scotland.
TO PUT ON ONE'S HOUNCES	Suffolk.
TO PUT ON ONE'S JOURNEY HARNESS	Dorset.
horse brasses	the common name applied to those brasses hung on the leather, as well as the general terms for all brass decorations.
BREAST PIECES	Hampson & Scott catalogue.
DROPS	Newton's catalogue 1871.

FACE PIECES	Matthew Harvey catalogue 1883—general to the trade.
HANGING PIECES	R. E. Thacker catalogue 1895.
MEDALLIONS	N.W. England.
PLATES	south of England.
bearing rein	general over Britain.
BRIDLE REIN	Midlands.
HAME REIN	Midlands and S.W. England.
breastplate	the name preferred by most horsemen for the decorated strap between the collar and the girth. Also used by the trade.
BREAST GIRTH	S.E. England.
BREAST STRAP	S.W. England, mid and south Scotland.
CHEST PIECE	Sussex.
MARTINGALE	south Midlands, E. Anglia, N.E. England (from the false martingale used in driving harness).
face piece	in general use in England and Wales.
FACE BRASS	Shropshire.
FACE PLATE	Lancashire.
FACEN	Fifeshire, Stirlingshire.
FACINGS	N.E. Scotland.
FORE PLATE, BRASS	S.E. England.
FOREHEAD PIECE	Devonshire.
FOREHEAD PLATE	Shropshire.
HEAD PIECE	Shropshire.
SEREN	west Wales (seren=a star—the usual shape of a brass worn).
SWINGER	west Midlands.
fly head terret	see map fig. 43.
lead rein	general in southern half of England.
BEARING REIN	west Midlands.
CHECK REIN	Midlands.
CURB REIN	west Midlands.
SIDE REIN	southern England.
neck lace	S.E. England and E. Anglia.
BEARER	Kent.
NECK STRAP	south Midlands.
NECK THONG	Hampshire.

rein hanger	trade and common name for the decorated strap holding a metal ring through which the reins passed.
CARRYING STRAP	Midlands.
LEAD RUNNER	Sussex.
REIN BEARER	N.W. England.
REIN CARRIER	Shropshire.
RUNNER	Kent.

The decorations standing above the plaited mane, fashioned out of straw or wire and ribbon were:

FLAGS	general.
NOPPINS	N.W. England.
SPRIGS	S.W. Scotland.
STANDARDS	west Midlands.
TOSSLES	Midlands, eastern England.

Finally, when tying the horse up to its stall in the stable, the rope from the halter ran through a ring on the manger and a piece of wood or iron was tied to the end to act as a weight and to stop the rope pulling through the manger ring. This piece of wood or iron was known as:

BLOCK	Cornwall.
BUNNAN BALL	Morayshire.
CLOG	Yorkshire, N.W. England.
HELTER COB	northern England.
LOG	northern England, southern Scotland.
MANGER BALL	generally, especially by the trade.
MANGER LOG	trade catalogues.
NAGGER	Midlands.
NOG	Lincolnshire.
PLUG	Devonshire.
SINKER	N.E. Scotland, E. Anglia.
TOGGLE	Dumfries-shire.

APPENDIX ONE

A Wagoner's Year

Ron Creasey was one of the last horsemen to be trained on a big farm in Holderness during the early 1940s and was also one of the last to be hired at an annual hiring fair. In the following account he describes a typical year's work on one of these large arable farms just after the Second World War.

'We had horses longer than most districts and did not finish with them till the crawler tractor came. We did have an odd tractor in 1937 but on this strong land the horse was unbeaten.

'I must start at dinnertime on the 23rd of November, the starting day of what we called Martinmass Week, when we received our year's pay and left our places if we weren't stopping again. On the Tuesday following, we went to get hired for the following year. Having been looked over as we stood in the Hull streets and been hired, we went to our new places on the coming Sunday. We were hired to do and work the horses and to live and eat in the foreman's house, or hind house, as it was known.

'All places of any consequence were staffed similar. There was a foreman, wagoner, third lad, fourth lad and so on, depending on the number of horses on the farm. There was also a head labourer and other labourers, a stockman ("bullocky") and also a "Tommy Owt" (an odd job man able to turn his hand to anything about the farm). Most farms had sheep; we had a flock of 400 ewes, but the foreman and the master shepherded between them.

'The wagoner and lads arrived at the foreman's house on Sunday night, depending on how far they had come. Twenty miles is a fair bike ride, with a big case and working top coat on your handlebars! As soon as you arrived, you would be shown your horses.

'Our horses were in two lots. The wagoner was responsible for feeding eight horses and mucking out two. The third and fourth lads also had to feed eight horses and muck out two. Each man had two lads to muck out the other six horses.

'At 5.30 a.m. on the Monday morning the foreman shouted us all up. The wagoner and two more were allowed stable lamps upstairs. Within five minutes of the foreman shouting, I reckoned to have two horses fed. As we went downstairs we would hear him say: "Gear them all for wagons; wag" (wag was a common abbreviation for wagoner in east Yorkshire). That meant that all the horses had to have collars and back-band traces on (east York-shire wagons were provided with poles, not shafts).

'A whistle blew to let us know when breakfast was ready. After a quick wash—all in the same water—we were back in the stable at about ten minutes to seven to plait the horse's tails up. By this time all the labourers had also come in to the stable to hear the foreman give his orders. "Five pairs in wagons for carting straw for bedding up the bullocks, the labourers to fork the straw; three pairs in wagons for mangolds" (which were thrown on the straw after the bullocks had been bedded). Bullocky and some other labourers cut up turnips in the turnip cutter for the fat bullocks.

'About eight o'clock, when all was done, all horsemen went off to plough and labourers to hedge and dyke. The foreman and wagoner set out all the rigs, 30 yards apart, whilst the third lad finished all furrows and the rest ploughed one after the other—"fox hounding", we called it. When all the rigs had been set, the foreman would then plough with us, and when we had got plough up (the whole farm ploughed) and after a good frost, some of us would start to quart, or cross-plough or turn furrows back.

'In between the ploughing we had forty days threshing wheat, barley, oats, peas and beans. The wagoner was expected to carry all corn—wheat in 18 stone sacks, barley 16 stone, and oats in 12 stone sacks. Third lad to carry when threshing spring corn and a labourer to help when threshing winter corn. (To be a wagoner in Holderness you not only had to be a good horseman, but a good weight lifter too!) All this had been agreed at the hiring in Hull.

'Some of the corn was put straight on the wagons to be taken to the nearest railway station, the foreman riding on the first wagon. As always, he would stand on the wagon shears (shafts), and the wagoner and the three main lads followed in their wagons.

'We also had 1000 tons of potatoes to be riddled during the winter. With spring just round the corner, all available horses were got up. Tommy Owt came into the stable and the lads each had more horses to attend to. The foreman would start to break in four or five young horses.

'We would start to drill slag for the peas, three drills with two horses in each; start to harrow the ploughing with several sets of three horse gibb harrows, each set harrowing 13 acres a day, four horse sets harrowing 16 acres a day and harrowing wheat with wood harrows at 22 acres a day. After it had been harrowed to the master's liking, we would start to drill at 20 acres a day. The boy who harrowed the seeds in had to fill up the scuttles (two-handled bins which were used to fill the seeder) each time they were empty. The men drilling would keep the drills themselves filled. The boss would come on his hunting horse, his words, as always; "Walk 'em on, walk 'em on; it will soon be night."

'Next we would be making potato rows, five acres a day for a pair of horses pulling a rowing plough. Schoolboys planted the potatoes with buckets.

'All men and horses were now working the land. The foreman and Tommy Owt were busy lambing. Bullocky had to manage to get his own straw and mangolds for 300 bullocks with the help of only one boy. We grew 20 acres of mangolds and varying acres of swedes each year.

'The horses were now going out to work again at six in the evenings till eight or nine at night. If it rained and we could not get on the land, we would all help with the sheep and cattle.

'When the corn was all sown up we rolled it with a cambridge roll, at 20 acres a day. All the corn was shimmed (the soil between the rows disturbed) by horse hoes, ten rows at a time, 20 acres a day. All the labourers followed with hoes to remove weeds.

'Next followed a month of muck leading (taking the muck and straw from the bullock yards to a muck hill in the fields) using seven or eight wagons, with four men filling and one helping to team (empty) at the muck hill. When we mucked fallows, roads had first to be ploughed across the fields, for it was too rough otherwise for the horses and wagons. The furrows were ploughed at equal distances so we could spread as far as each other's wagon.

'When hay time came, with four pairs of horses we cut 24 acres a day using two reapers. The hay was turned till dry and then cocked (built in small stacks) by hand. Later the hay was brought to the stacks, built by the foreman and the head labourer.

'At harvest time we used four or five binders, four horses to each binder. Two men were kept busy bringing fresh horses and taking tired ones home. The men who rode the binders were also the men who stacked the sheaves, with one exception; the boss rode one of the binders. The foreman, wagoner, head labourer, and sometimes Tommy Owt, rode the others. At the same time, the grass reapers were cutting the 100 acres of peas.

'When we started harvesting we would get a lot of casual labour. At one time it was all Irish, who came and lived on the place for the harvest month. I have seen forty pairs of men stooking in one field and five stacks going up at once. Four pair of horses were needed to keep each stack going.

'Potato picking followed harvest, with three horses yoked abreast to a potato spinner and five or six horses in carts to move the potatoes picked up from each of two spinners. After the potatoes came the mangolds, or wusels, as we used to call them. Only seven pairs of

horses in carts were needed for this, the rest were ploughing and
sowing wheat all on the same day. This was sown on a one year
white clover ley solely for the sheep to graze.

'As there wasn't much time left before winter came, it was
possible we would have nine pairs ploughing; three horses in a
roller, covering nine furrows at a time; three horses following with
a set of gibb harrows; two horses with a drill, sowing artificial
(fertiliser), followed by another three with a second set of gibb
harrows; two horses pulling the corn drill, and the seeds were
covered by three horses pulling another set of gibb harrows, followed, finally, by a pair of horses with straight-toothed harrows.
If the harrows caught up the ploughing they wouldn't stop, but
would go back over what they had already covered, even three times
if necessary.

'By this time it was getting dark around 4.30 p.m. so we would
have short days. Also, it was getting near to the 23rd November
and we were getting ready for some money. The boss, or foreman
would come round and ask if we would stop again. They would ask
each week for about three weeks, during which you would air your
grievances and maybe if one lad was not stopping, you would step
up one. If they did not want anyone, they just didn't ask him, so
you knew that if the others had been asked and not you, you were
not wanted and would have to go to Hull again to be hired.'

It seems incredible to learn that up to twenty years ago, these
wagoners on the big farms around Holderness were still being
hired by the year. Once they had accepted the hiring fee, or 'fastening
fee'—from five shillings to one pound—they were more or less
bound to their employer. They were expected to be single and had
to live in the foreman's house, where they went only to wash, eat
and sleep.

If they wanted to get married during the year, they had to live
apart from their wives and then, at the end of the year, if they
could not get a foreman's job, they would have to go as farm labourers
—who were weekly paid and not expected to live in.

For the extra hour at each end of the day spent tending their
horses, they received £12.10s. per annum, which worked out at
sixpence per hour overtime. (At the same time even the labourers
were receiving nearly five shillings an hour for overtime.)

They had to be on time for their meals, or go without. All their
food and bed was provided as part of the hiring, and to keep them
in pocket money, they were allowed five shillings each week 'beside
our plate' by way of sub money.

When the big farms finally gave up the horses, the hiring system
came to an end.

Some Old Horse Recipes

Bill Laker, like Ron Creasey, one of the last of the breed of trained horsemen, was given the following recipes by an old Oxfordshire carter. Many of them read like something one would expect to find in a book on witchcraft. Few of the ingredients are to be found today in a modern dictionary—let alone a chemists shop in the High Street.

OILS TO MANAGE A RESTIVE HORSE

        oil of myrtistica   ½ dram
        oil of duty   1 dram
        oil of man   2 dram

Mix together, then put a few drops on the horse's tongue and rub a little on your hands for him to smell.

TO CATCH ANY VICIOUS HORSE or WILD COLT

Sweat a piece of bread under your arm, scent it with oil of vidgin and oil of fermse. Get the wind so that the horse can smell it; you will be able to approach him and give him a piece, which will gentle him.

OILS to STOP a KICKER

        oil of ben
        oil of duty
        oil of burdock
        oil of man
        oil of Exeter

Equal parts—put a few drops on the nose and tongue.

BROKEN KNEE OINTMENT—to make the hair grow

        blue ointment   2 oz
        honey   1 oz
        powdered charcoal ½ dram
        oil of Rosemary   1 dram

Mix well together and apply twice a day.

OIL TO MAKE A MARE COVER

        powdered valerian root
        powdered damiana leaves

hypophosphite of calcium
powdered grains of paradise
saccharated carbonate of iron

Equal parts are mixed and one tablespoonful is given every night in corn, for fourteen days before the time.

OIL TO MAKE A LEAN HORSE FAT

capsicine	5 drops
oil of sweet flag	$\frac{1}{4}$ oz
oil of cassia	1 dram
oil of chamamiles	1 dram
oil of coriander	$\frac{1}{4}$ oz
oil of allspice	$\frac{1}{4}$ oz

Mix a quarter teaspoonful with a little sugar and give with corn every night.

Bill Laker's own recipe for keeping horses fit and well:
'good feeding
good grooming
patience
kindness and understanding

Mix well and you'll find it to be the best medicine for the most patient and faithful friend a man could have—the heavy horse!'

Bibliography

ALISON, E. V.   'Brass Amulets' (Connoisseur, October 1911)

ARNOLD, J.   *The Shell Book of Country Crafts* (John Baker, 1968)

BIDDELL, H., and others   *Heavy Horse Breeds and Management* (Vinton, 1919)

BROWN, R. A.   *Horse Brasses* (W, H. Allen, 1963)

CARTER, H. R.   'English Horse Amulets' (Connoisseur, July 1916)
'The Age of Horse Brasses' (Connoisseur, 1931)

CHILDE, V. G.   'Wheeled Vehicles' *A History of Technology* (Singer, Holmyard and Hall, Vol. 1, Oxford, 1954)

ECKENSTEIN, LINA   'Horse Brasses' (Reliquary and Illustrated Archeologist, 1906)

EVANS, EWART   *Ask the Fellows Who Cut The Hay* (Faber, 1962)
The Horse in the Furrow (Faber, 1960)

Farm Horses   Young Farmers Club Booklet No. 13 (Evans, 1951)

GORDON, W. J.   *The Horse World of London (1893)* (David and Charles, reprint 1971)

HARTFIELD, G.   *Horse Brasses* (Abelard-Schuman, 1965)

HASLUCK, Paul N.   *Saddlery and Harness-Making* (J, A. Allen, reprint 1962)

HUGHES, G. B.   *Horse Brasses and other Small Items For the Collector* (Country Life, 1964)

JENKINS, J. GERAINT   *Agricultural Transport in Wales* (Welsh Folk Museum, 1962)
Traditional Country Craftsmen (Routledge and Kegan Paul, 1965)

JOPE, E. M.   'Vehicles and Harness', *A History of Technology Vol. 2* (Oxford, 1954)

RICHARDS, H. S.   *All About Horse Brasses* (Drew and (Hopwood, 1970)
Horse Brass Collections Nos. 1, 2 and 3 (Drew and Hopwood, 1970)

Saddlery and Harness   Monthly Pub. T. Kirby; Walsall 1891–1930
SIDNEY, S.   *The Book of the Horse* (Cassell, 1878)
Standard Cyclopedia of Modern Agriculture   Ed. Prof. Sir Robert Wright (Gresham, 1911)
STEPHENS, H.   *The Book of the Farm* (Blackie, 2nd Ed., 1849)
TYLDEN, G.   *Discovering Harness and Saddlery* (Shire, 1971)
VESEY-FITZGERALD, B.   Ed., *The Book of the Horse* (Nicholson and Watson, 1954)
VINCE, John   *Discovering Horse Brasses* (Shire, 1970)
WRIGHT, REV. P.   *Salute the Carthorse* (Ian Allen, 1971)
YOUATT, W.   *The Horse* (Longmans, 1851)

Acknowledgements

I would like to thank all those who made the collecting of material for this book so enjoyable. I have mentioned most of those who supplied me with information during the course of the book, but I would also like to thank those not specifically mentioned. Those who answered my questionnaires by post; those who talked to me at the bar of country inns up and down the country; those who invited me into their homes just for the sheer joy of talking about the heavy horses; those who made arrangements for me to visit the right people; to them all I say 'thank you from the bottom of my heart'. The past two years have given me some of the most wonderful moments in my life.

To the museum staffs who have helped me in my researches I am greatly indebted, particularly to the staff of the Leathercraft Museum at Walsall and the Museum of English Rural Life at Reading.

I am indebted too to the horsemen who allowed me to watch them at work at the shows, and also to the companies still working the horses who have entertained me at their stables. I am particularly grateful to those manufacturers in Walsall who allowed me to visit their premises and in many cases to borrow valuable sources of material.

It is difficult to single out one name above any other, but I must particularly thank Ron Creasey for all his hard work and particularly for his account of a wagoner's year; Bill Laker for his long correspondence and permission to print his collection of horsemen's recipes; and finally Walter Fisher who supplied me with some wonderful sketches, many of which have formed the basis of the drawings in the text.

I am greatly indebted to my brother Geoff for his work on the drawings, and to all those who have loaned photographs.

Most of all I wish to express my sincere thanks to Dorian Williams for introducing me to the world of writing books and to my publishers for their faith in my ability to produce a book worthy of their attention.

Finally, whilst every effort has been made to trace owners of copyright material, if any have been inadvertently overlooked, this error will be corrected in any future editions.

Index

End pages—Face piece and fly head terret patterns from the
1895 catalogue of R. E. Thacker, Walsall

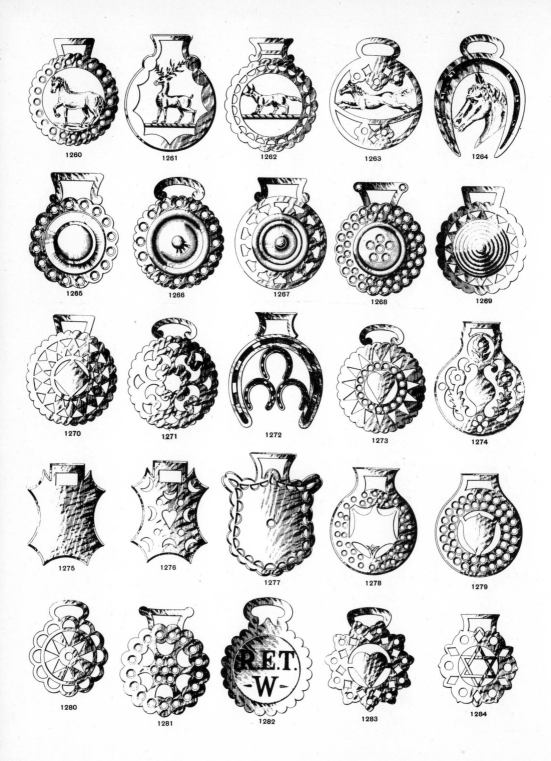

1260 1261 1262 1263 1264

1265 1266 1267 1268 1269

1270 1271 1272 1273 1274

1275 1276 1277 1278 1279

1280 1281 1282 1283 1284